THE STORY OF
LAXEY
FLOUR

Laxey and Lonan Heritage Trust

Officers and Management Committee

Laxey and Lonan Heritage Trust, Newsletter 30

This edition of the Laxey and Lonan Heritage Trust Newsletter has been published jointly with The Manx Experience and Laxey Glen Mills Ltd to celebrate 150 years of milling at the Laxey Glen Mill. The usual articles, features and news items will appear in Newsletter 31 which will be issued shortly.

THE STORY OF LAXEY FLOUR

150 memorable years of
Laxey Flour Mill
Isle of Man

Andrew Scarffe

Published by
THE MANX EXPERIENCE in conjunction with LAXEY GLEN MILLS
and with the assistance of LAXEY & LONAN HERITAGE TRUST
to commemorate the
150th Anniversary of Laxey Glen Mills - 1860 - 2010

To Nichola, Francesca and Bethany

ACKNOWLEDGEMENTS

The publication of this commemorative booklet would not have been possible without the generous support and assistance of numerous individuals and organisations.

The Laxey and Lonan Heritage Trust publish a forty-eight page newsletter three times each year and it had been the intention to issue a special newsletter commemorating the Mill's 150th anniversary. With the enthusiastic and financial support of Laxey Glen Mill Ltd and in particular its chairman Colin Brown, the opportunity was taken to publish a proper commemorative booklet. Colin also undertook the tasks of typesetting and editing the booklet.

Sandra Donnelly, miller and manager, has also given enthusiastic support to the project. She has patiently answered innumerable questions about the milling process and checked the subsequent text for accuracy. Her limitless enthusiasm and interest in all aspects of the Mill was evident during my numerous visits.

Much of the historical information on which this book has been based has been sourced from the Archives and Library of Manx National Heritage. My grateful thanks to Library and Archive Services Officer Paul Weatherall and his staff for their assistance, in particular with allowing permission to photograph Robert Casement's 1858 drawing of the Mill and for access to the vehicle registration records. Patricia Newton generously shared the results of her own research into the Mill's history. Compilation of the recent history was greatly assisted by the use of notes and photographs which were compiled by the late Nigel Mahoney.

Derek Osborn provided a wealth of information and clarification of the improvements and changes made to the Mill which he planned and carried out during his time as miller and manager. John Kneale provided fascinating recollections of his many years' employment at the Mill; he began work there in 1942 at the age of 14. Albert Fleming, who also worked at the Mill for over 40 years, provided confirmation of details of the Mill's history. Bob Kinrade provided information regarding the building work which his father in law, Edwin Kneale, had carried out to the Mill, together with information about the grain deliveries. Malcolm Quirk and Willie Callister provided names for all those on the 1981 staff photograph.

Michael Leece kindly checked the vehicle fleet list and provided details (and some fascinating photographs) of vehicles which I had omitted. John Guest, Peter Maggs, Arthur Kinrade and Ken Kinrade provided additional information regarding the vehicles.

Stan Basnett, Stuart Bridson, Willie Callister, Mark Edwards, Mike Kelly, John Kneale, George Lawson, Michael Leece, Brian McMullen, Chris Wedgwood and Manx National Heritage kindly loaned or allowed the use of photographs from their collections. Those photographs not credited in the captions were provided by the Mill.

Andrew Scarffe, May 2010

Printed by Mannin Media Limited : Douglas : Isle of Man

FOREWORD

by Speaker of the House of Keys
and Chairman of the
Laxey and Lonan Heritage Trust
Hon Steve Rodan

The history of Laxey Glen Mills over the last 150 years is very much the story of Laxey and its people. This superbly illustrated book "The Story of Laxey Flour" by Laxey historian Andrew Scarffe tells that story magnificently.

The shaping of the Mill by the personalities involved and vagaries of business are all traced in what is an absorbing read – as well as carefully researched historical, technical and social record.

Once there were 50 flour mills on the Island – today only Laxey Glen Mills remains in production. From beginnings in 1861 – the creation of Richard Rowe and Robert Casement of Great Laxey Wheel fame – the Mill has produced not only wheat flour, but semolina, soda bread flour and animal feed.

This is also a story of Victorian turbines powered by river water, of horse-drawn carts, steam wagons and gas engines; of grain boats at Laxey harbour, and flour conveyed to Douglas by the M.E.R.; and of steady technological advance.

It is also a story of disastrous fires, strikes, intense commercial competition from imported flour and bread; of 24-hour working during the war effort; of threatened closure, and political intervention.

Owned and managed for 100 years by generations of the Corlett family until ultimate nationalisation in 1974, the Mill was directly responsible for the employment of 40 people with their families in Laxey.

Today, as a profitable concern, 30 tonnes of quality flour is produced each week for the Island's needs or exported to specialist bakers in England. Around 150 individuals and families – farmers, bakers and Mill operatives – still rely for their livelihood on Laxey Glen Mills. As the Island's only producer of flour from locally grown wheat it can proudly claim to be key to our self sufficiency in food.

"The Story of Laxey Flour" is fitting tribute to Laxey Glen Mills and the men and women connected with it over the past century and a half. In this 150th Anniversary year, my very best wishes in the years ahead.

CONTENTS

—— 1 ——

IN THE BEGINNING

Many thousands of years ago our distant ancestors, the first primitive human beings, gathered seeds from plants and after removing the outer skins, chewed and ate the inner raw kernel. This is probably how man first came to eat grains, which are the edible seeds of certain types of grass plants and include millet, oats, barley, rye, maize, corn and wheat and commonly known as cereals, the name being derived from the Roman god Ceres, the protector of grain. Archaeological evidence indicates that early man developed from being gatherers to farmers by cultivating these grains some 10,000 years ago.

Today, wheat is the most widely grown of these grains and it is thought to have originated and been first cultivated in the Tigris and Euphrates river valleys close to the area now known as Iraq. Wheat probably developed from the accidental cross breeding of wild grasses. It is thought that it was first ground and mixed with water to form dough and then baked to form primitive breads some 8000 years ago. Wheat and bread are both recorded in 5000-year-old Egyptian tombs; the Chinese were cultivating wheat at a similar time period. It first reached Britain in about 2000 BC but it wasn't until the mid-eighteenth century that it was introduced to North America. Like many of mankind's discoveries, the processes of making flour and bread were probably first made by a combination of accident and experimentation.

Once man had learnt how to cultivate and store grain he did not have to lead a nomadic existence in order to find food and was able to settle and live in a fixed community. The cultivation of grain has therefore lead directly to the societies and cultures in which we all live today.

Bread is thus one of the earliest known prepared foods and has been a staple part of mankind's diet since these ancient times. It remains today a basic foodstuff through almost all cultures through-out the world. It is deeply rooted in many cultures and religions, for example in the Holy Communion and Christianity. The term has crept into our common language; "bread" as slang to denote belongings and money or a "bread winner" to denote a wage earner.

In the United Kingdom, ninety nine per cent of households buy and consume bread of varying types. Every day, approximately ten million large loaves of bread are baked and the equivalent of 220 million slices of bread are eaten. Bread is an extremely healthy food; it is not fattening, it provides protein, iron, Vitamin B and carbohy-drates and is a good source of iron. And can there be a more pleasant smell than that of warm freshly baked bread?

Milling and baking, the processes by which bread is made, are therefore amongst the oldest of skills and trades still practiced by man today. Throughout this time span of many thousands of years the basic principle of milling, the reduction of grains into flour, has remained unchanged. Stone Age man pounded grain between stones by hand; modern milling techniques use rollers to reduce the grain into its components.

Gradually man developed more efficient ways of milling. Simple pounding between stones gave way to properly shaped stones known as querns. Although in a number of different forms, querns consist-ed of a fixed base stone and an upper stone that rubbed against it; some of these were disc shaped stones or others were in the form of a rolling pin.

These early forms of grinding stone gradually gave way to the familiar mill stones, two large disc shaped stones where the upper stone, known as the runner, turned against a stationary lower or base stone. Grooves, to varying patterns, were cut into the faces of the stones so that when grain was fed in through a hole in middle of the runner stone, the resultant flour would be forced outwards from between the stones as they were turned. The grooves were cut into the stones by an extremely skilled trade know as dressing. A later improvement was the ability to raise or lower the upper stone to adjust the coarseness of the flour, which was then fed through sieves to obtain whiter flour.

The upper stone was turned by human or animal power but the harnessing of waterpower with the use of waterwheels has variously been attributed to the Greeks or Romans in about 300BC. The water-wheel was set either horizontally or, much more commonly, vertically and would be powered with water collected from an adjacent river in a water course or trough commonly known as a race or lade. A series of shafts and cogs connected to the waterwheel turned the millstones and other ancillary machinery in the mill. Water mills quickly spread throughout Britain but it wasn't until the twelfth century that windmills were built for the first time. Reliant on an intermittent form of energy, windmills would not become as widespread as watermills. During medieval times, the nobility increasingly demanded whiter and purer flour as brown wholemeal flour was seen as the preserve of the poorer classes. Today it is recognised that invariably brown breads are a healthier option.

In 1878, roller mills were introduced to Britain and revolutionised flour milling. Invented by Henry Simon a Swiss engineer, roller mills used a principle of "gradual reduction" whereby grain was reduced to its component parts in a series of stages using rollers. The system

Ballacowle Corn Mill on the Agneash Road photographed in the early 1950s. Although by this time the mill had been converted into a small engineering works, it was still possible to operate the waterwheel which once powered the mill machinery

Photo collection, Andrew Scarffe

resulted in increased flour production, whiter flour and cheaper bread. As demand for whiter flour spread across the country, mills faced a choice of either investing in new roller technology or attempting to survive producing lower grade flour. Roller mills were to prompt the decline and almost total extinction of the traditional British water mill.

Milling on the Isle of Man was to follow a similar evolutionary process, from crushing grain by hand through to the introduction of roller mills. The earliest water powered mills had small horizontal wheels with paddles and were known as "myllen beg" or "little mills". These gradually gave way to mills with larger vertical waterwheels which were commonly known as cornmills, although the term corn in this sense was a generic term used to describe all the grains which were milled.

From the early fifteenth century, under the rule of the Island by the Stanleys and later the Athols, the use of private individual watermills were banned and farmers were required to take their grain to the Lord's mills to be ground. Farmers were told which mill to use, had to pay for its use and also could be called upon to contribute to its upkeep; it was in effect a form of tithe. Querns were ordered to be destroyed but this proved difficult to enforce in the more remote areas. By the mid nineteenth century control of the Lords over milling had ceased by which time there were over 50 mills on the Island. There had been a brief but unsuccessful flirtation with windmills, notably in Ramsey and Castletown.

A new chapter in the Manx milling history began in 1860 with the opening of the Laxey Glen Mill. Originally using the traditional millstones, the mill was constructed on a much grander and larger scale than the traditional mills with a consequently increased production capacity. It was one of only two Manx mills to change to the roller system. Gradually, the traditional mills closed. Today, only the Laxey Glen Mill remains in production.

CENTURY OF DEVELOPMENT

The village of Laxey derives its name from a Scandinavian term meaning Salmon River. It was named by the Vikings who discovered a small community living near where the salmon filled river flowed into the large bay. The inhabitants fished from the bay and farmed from small crofts dotted around the steep slopes of the valley sides and hills. It was to remain this way for centuries.

The village of Laxey derives its name from a Scandinavian term meaning Salmon River. It was named by the Vikings who discovered a small community living near where the salmon-filled river flowed into the large bay. The inhabitants fished from the bay and farmed from small crofts dotted around the steep slopes of the valley sides and hills. It was to remain this way for centuries.

In 1797, a visitor to Laxey noted that it *"is a group of about thirty cottages, in a deep glen, opening into a fine bay on one side, and surrounded by steep and lonely mountains. It has a herring-house, at present unemployed; also a flax-mill, a tucking-mill, and three corn-mills."*

A few years later, in 1811 another visitor noted that *"Laxey is a place of little trade, being composed of not more than thirty cottages. It has only one shop, apparently very ill supplied, and two public houses. For butcher's meat and many other articles of convenience the inhabitants send weekly to Douglas. A little way up the valley is a flax-spinning mill"* .

A packhorse road linking Douglas and Ramsey passed down each side of the valley, paying scant respect to the steep gradients, to a small bridge over the river adjacent to a public house. Travel along the road was difficult and slow at all times of the year; dusty and dry and summer and a muddy quagmire in winter.

This was all to change with the discovery of rich deposits of lead ore beneath the hills and valleys. The first mining trial began in about

1780 but it wasn't until the early 1820s that mining began in earnest and when production peaked in 1875, 2400 tons of lead ore and 11753 tons of zinc were produced, the latter accounting for nearly half of the UK total output of zinc that year. In 1850 the Laxey Mining Company had began the construction of the Laxey Wheel to pump floodwater from the mines workings. Set in motion on 27th September, 1854 and named the *Lady Isabella* it was the largest water-wheel in the world. Following a slow and relentless decline,the mine finally closed in 1929. Fortunately the *Lady Isabella* was saved by Laxey builder Edwin Kneale and today, under the ownership of Manx National Heritage, it still turns during the summer season for the enjoyment of the many tourists who come to Laxey.

At the beginning of January, 1845 the Laxey Mining Company advertised for a new manager, who had to be "a practical miner" and who would be paid a salary which would "place him above the temp-tation of receiving bribes". Within a month Richard Rowe, a Cornishman had been appointed. His name would quickly become synonymous with the Great Laxey Mine in particular and with the Manx mining industry in general. Described as a great mining engi-neer, there were few Manx mines which were not eager at some time to associate themselves with his name. Rowe also showed himself to be a philanthropist and entrepreneur, quickly becoming involved in many aspects of the community and business life of Laxey. He was

The village of Laxey and its Bay as depicted in this impression by J Murkill published by J Mylrea in 1857.

Photo,
The Manx Experience

closely involved with Laxey School, the Working Men's Institute and Christ Church. He constructed a brewery, had shipping interests, led the fundraising to repair Laxey harbour and constructed the Laxey Glen Flour Mill. However, much of Rowe's activities are shrouded in an air of mystery and little is known of his seemingly complex financial arrangements. In contrast to his public image, in reality many of his business ventures proved to be less than profitable; almost all of the mines in which he was involved, with the exception of Great Laxey, were financial failures to varying extents.

Richard Rowe was born in 1823 in St Agnes, a notable tin mining area of Cornwall, to a family with a mining background. He was only 22 years old when appointed as Captain, a Cornish term to describe the mine manager, of Great Laxey. His appointment was recommended by a shareholder, George Dumbell, who it would seem was already well acquainted with Rowe through mining interests in Northern Ireland. Dumbell was appointed Chairman of the mining company in 1849 and thereafter dominated the affairs of the mine (and many other Manx businesses as well) until his death in 1887. His name is remembered in Manx history due to the collapse of the bank bearing his name in 1900. Rowe was to become one of Dumbell's closest lieutenants and there are suggestions that Dumbell privately financed some of the enterprises in which Rowe was involved.

Following Rowe's appointment as mine Captain, and at Dumbell's instigation, there followed a period of investment at the mine culminating in 1854 with the completion of the Laxey Wheel *Lady Isabella*.

During the 1860s, there was considerable criticism of Rowe's management of the mine but these were largely ignored as huge profits were made. The criticisms did not prevent him from becoming one of the first two popularly elected MHKs for Garff sheading in 1867. Rowe eventually resigned as mine Captain in the midst of allegations of mismanagement towards the end of the 1872 miners strike and took up residence in Douglas. In the midst of this, at times, turbulent period, Rowe somehow managed to find the time and energy to construct the Laxey Glen Mill. It is the only one of his business ventures which still survives in active operation today.

The rapid expansion of the Great Laxey Mine was reflected in an equally rapid expansion of the population of the parish of Lonan, within which the village is situated, as men and their families moved to Laxey to seek employment in the mine. In 1792 Lonan had a population of 1408; by 1871 this had risen to 3741. During the 1870s, nearly 800 people were employed at the mine. A staple part of the community's diet was bread and presumably there were concerns about the existing mills' ability to provide sufficient flour for the increasing population. Although little is known about the early industrial archaeology of Laxey, there were at least three corn mills in the area at this time although only one, Creer's or Ballacowle Mill situated at the foot of the steep road leading to the hamlet of Agneash, appears to have been in active production. The mill last worked in 1939 and shortly after the end of the Second World War it was converted into a small engineering works by Manx Engineers Ltd. Moughtins Mill, situated on the confluence of the Laxey and Glen Roy rivers, was incorporated into the St George's Woollen Mill, when the latter opened in 1881. Both of these early mills were of the traditional type, powered by a small water wheel. The location of the third corn mill is not known with any certainty. Another mill was located at Garwick some two miles south of Laxey and was known as the Ballagawne Mill. Towards the end of the 1850s, with concerns about the adequacy of the existing mills, Rowe decided to construct a new mill of a sufficient size and capacity to supply flour not only to Laxey but also to the rest of the Island.

One of the most interesting aspects of the Great Laxey Mine was the use of water power to operate the mining machinery. Although the use of water power in mining was widespread, at Laxey this was taken to an extreme and without parallel at any other mine in the British Isles. The mining company, as well as other local industries, constructed waterwheels, turbines and reservoirs and connected these with a system of water courses, similar to miniature canals, known as races or lades. Water was collected from one water wheel or turbine and conveyed in a lade directly to another waterwheel or turbine further down the valley, the water being used again and again as it flowed down to the sea. Almost every other small river was used by some industry dependent on its water. It was very difficult for any new industry to use water without impinging on other established uses.

The least used river was that flowing down from Glen Roy, although in 1853, water was diverted from the river near to its source by the Laxey Mine for use by the *Lady Isabella* waterwheel. This right had been secured in the early 1850s when Richard Rowe, acting on behalf of the mining company, had purchased a mill, cottage and lands in the Glen Roy valley. The object was to divert water from the river which also supplied the mill and avoid the payment of compensation to the mill owner. This is referred to in a deed dating to November, 1853 which records the sale by Rowe of the "dwelling house, mill cottage and lands, late the property Robert Corlett, dyer" to one William Hampton. The sale reserved to Rowe the right and title to the water of the stream which formerly supplied the mill.

The dye works referred to are believed to have been situated a short distance down valley of the present Laxey Glen Mill building and in the immediate vicinity of the present Manx Electric Railway viaduct. The mill mentioned in the deed may refer to the third corn mill mentioned earlier the location of which is otherwise unknown. It may therefore follow that there was an earlier corn mill on the site of the present Laxey Glen Mill.

With water rights secured, Rowe set about obtaining land suitable for the construction of the new mill. One of the few suitable locations in the Glen Roy valley was a piece of flat land on the western side of the river, at Laxey, just upstream from where Moore's viaduct carried the New Road, completed in 1854, across the valley.

In 1858, the Laxey Mining Company's engineer Robert Casement, who a few years earlier had designed and constructed the Laxey Wheel, prepared drawings for Rowe of the proposed layout of machinery inside the mill. There were to be four floors and a turbine, situated beneath the basement, was to power six pairs of grinding stones. The drawing records that the turbine was to operate at 400 to 500 revolutions per minute and would be geared through a number of bevel wheels so that the revolving grindstones would operate at a final speed of 140 revolutions per minute. Water for the turbine was col-

A water lade, known locally as the "mill race" was constructed to supply water from the Laxey river to the holding tank, known as a cistern.

Photo, Andrew Scarffe

lected in a circular cistern of stone construction situated on the valley side above the mill and which was fed by a supply lade from a weir on the Glen Roy river. (The cistern and much of the supply lade survives largely intact).

Construction of the mill was recorded as being in progress during 1860 and by 16th January, 1861 the *Mona's Herald* was able to record that a *"very extensive flour mill has been erected on the south side of Laxey Glen. The noble building presents a creditable specimen of substantial masonry and to visitors passing over the new bridge, an imposing appearance. We understand that neither labour or expense has been spared in this construction and that is being fitted up with all the most recent improvements in mill machinery. The mill will supply a want long felt in that locality and we believe it is the intention of the pro-*

15

The circular, stone built holding tank or cistern for the mill turbine, which was supplied by water from the mill race.

Photo, Andrew Scarffe

prietor not only to grind for the public but to sell flour, meal, provender etc whole-sale and retail; and it is rumoured at lower prices that the public there have been in the habit of paying for them. If this is true, the mill will not only prove a boon to the poor man, but an accommodation to the community at large".

Unfortunately, of the actual construction, almost nothing is known. The builder is believed to have been John James Moore of Baljean who had some years earlier in 1854 built the adjacent viaduct to carry the New Road across the valley. The walls were constructed with thin angular Manx slate roughly coarsed, oral tradition recording that this was sourced from the waste stone from the Laxey Mine. Another possible source for the stone was a quarry on Baljean farm owned Moore. The front elevation of the mill was constructed with seven window bays with arched tops; these are purely decorative and serve no practical function. Oral tradition maintains that these arches

The original drawing by Casement identifies the "mill stones" at the top right of the drawing and is signed by Casement (bottom right).

Photograph courtesy of Manx National Heritage.

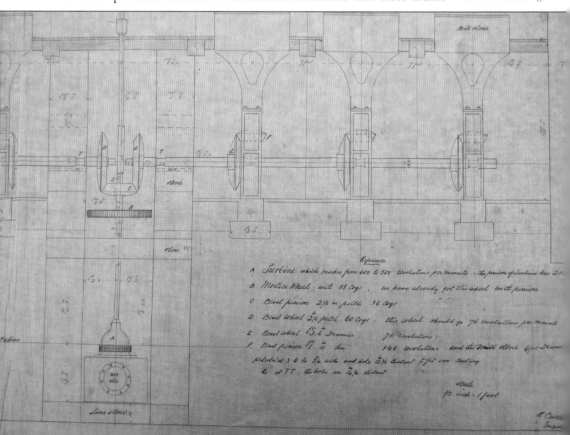

were incorporated by Robert Casement to replicate the row of arches which form the "rod duct" connected to the Laxey Wheel. The mill cistern was decorated with a similar embellishment.

An article published in 1893 noted that the mill was built by a Belfast firm but this may have been confused with MacAdam Brothers of the Soho Foundry in Belfast who supplied the turbine. MacAdams had by this time supplied at least one turbine to the

Laxey Mine which was used in the Machine House built in 1856. Both Rowe and Casement had visited the Soho Foundry in 1855 and it is assumed that Rowe was acquainted with the company through his Northern Ireland mining connections. It was recorded in 1876 that the cost of construction and subsequent capital outlay on buildings, machinery and warehouses etc., up to that time had been £10,000. It is not known how Rowe funded such costs although a deed dating to October, 1861 recorded the loan of £1000 from Rev Hugh Stowell Gill of Manchester to Rowe, with the Mill, buildings and land as security. Such loans may have been typical.

Richard Rowe, (top right) appointed Captain of Laxey Mines aged 22, swiftly established himself within the village community as a popular personality.

Photo collection,
Andrew Scarffe

Rowe secured the services of Robert Casement (right), who was engineer in charge of the construction of "Lady Isabella", to design and oversee the building of the mill.

Photo collection,
Andrew Scarffe

The mill was officially opened on 27th February, 1861 and the celebrations were typical of the time, with

17

LAXEY GLEN FLOUR MILLS,
(ERECTED 1862)

a "sumptuous repast" provided for the invited guests and a "treat" for the workmen followed by music from the Laxey Brass Band. During the afternoon, the invited guests assembled at the mill to witness the first official milling of flour. On the second floor, the guests were surprised to discover that Captain Rowe's *"domestics were busy preparing and laying out a substantial English dinner of roast beef and plum pudding"*. Rowe told the guests that *"his object being to supply a want generally felt, he had spared no expense to produce the very best article for the public and he would assure them in his future dealings, although looking for a return of his capital, still selfishness would not characterize his proceedings"*. The guests were invited to view the turbine and the mill machinery which included silk dressing machines, the first time these were used on the Island. Samples of the freshly produced flour elicited "the admiration of its judges". It was noted that steam power would shortly be added to the mill.

Amongst the many toasts proposed was one to the recently appointed "young miller" but who was not actually named in the newspaper report. As construction of the flour mill progressed, Rowe had advertised for a miller to operate it on his behalf. From over one hundred applicants Thomas Corlett, a young Manxman, was quickly offered the position. Thus began the Corlett family's connection with the mill which would last for nearly one hundred years.

One of the earliest known illustrations of the mill, believed to date to the late 1860s. The cistern is clearly visible on the left of the picture and a small water-wheel, its use being unknown, can be seen on the front of the screen house. Development of the Laxey Glen Gardens, to the rear of the mill, has yet to begin.

Photo, Collection Andrew Scarffe.

Thomas Corlett was born in Ballaugh in 1831 where his parents farmed at Corvalley. His milling career began when he was apprenticed to a Mr Glashen of Sulby and subsequently with a Mr Kerruish at Milntown. A move to Liverpool followed where, for a few years, he worked in a number of mills before deciding to emigrate to America. With the voyage booked, Corlett boarded the ship but found as a result of confusion with his bookings, his intended berth had already been filled. He returned ashore and home to the Isle of Man where he shortly afterwards began work with Mr Monks at the Wind Mill in Ramsey and married Catherine Stephen of Ballaugh. After successfully responding to Captain Rowe's advert, he was appointed miller at the Laxey Glen Mill at the age of 29.

Widely respected throughout the Island for his milling and business skills, Thomas Corlett ensured that the continued operation of the Laxey Glen Mill by investing in new milling technology when many other mills were closing due to the competition from cheaper imported flour. He also became closely involved with the local community, being an official of the Wesleyan Methodist circuit and a member of the House of Keys for Garff from 1891 until 1908.

Although Laxey has had a close affinity with the sea since early times, harbour protection for the small boats sailing from Laxey was rudimentary. Many had been wrecked by the fierce storms which blow into the bay during the winter months.

Thomas Corlett was a mere 29 years old when Rowe appointed him Miller at Laxey.

Photo, collection John Kneale.

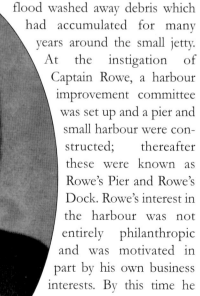

During December, 1860 a severe flood washed away debris which had accumulated for many years around the small jetty. At the instigation of Captain Rowe, a harbour improvement committee was set up and a pier and small harbour were constructed; thereafter these were known as Rowe's Pier and Rowe's Dock. Rowe's interest in the harbour was not entirely philanthropic and was motivated in part by his own business interests. By this time he

19

had already a financial interest in at least one vessel, a schooner named *Maria* which was used to carry general cargoes to the Island. In 1864 Rowe purchased the screw steamer *Chieftain* of which it was noted *"he intends chiefly for his own accommodation arising out of the increased traffic of the mill and also for the use of other persons who may patronise the vessel"*. *Chieftain* sailed primarily between Laxey, Liverpool and Whitehaven. During 1865, Rowe constructed a large four-floored warehouse on the quayside adjacent to the small dock ostensibly for use as a grain store for the flour mill, the work again being carried out by Moore of Baljean. In practice, however, the warehouse was used for a variety of purposes including the storage of ore for the mining company and, on the top

floor, as a place of entertainment where charitable events were held. During 1869, a warehouse on North Quay, Douglas was also purchased and a third in Ramsey was obtained a few years later; these two warehouses were primarily for the storage and retail of the mill's products. Following Rowe's death in 1886, the Laxey warehouse was acquired by Henry Bloom Noble in 1888. Thomas Corlett unsuccessfully attempted to buy the warehouse in 1905 for use by the mill. Subsequently passing through a number of owners over many years, the warehouse was more popularly known as the Pipe Factory, until the company ceased trading in 2002. It is now the home of the Mining Machinery Development Group.

During the hot summer months of the early 1860s, the Glen Roy River regularly dried to little more than a small trickle. As the mill was entirely dependent on the turbine to operate the machinery, milling was frequently interrupted due to the scarcity of water. To overcome this, a 40HP condensing steam engine was installed as an auxiliary power source and a large brick chimney was constructed at the rear of the mill. The steam engine was in use by 1866 although one source records that it was installed during the second year of the mill's operation.

By the early 1870s, in common with all other mills on the Island, the Laxey Glen Mill began to suffer from competition caused by imported flour from English mills. The situation was not helped when in June, 1872 the Laxey miners began a strike over pay which was to last until the end of the following October. During the strike, allegations were again made about Rowe's mismanagement of the mine. An investigation by the Directors into book keeping discrepancies resulted in their decision to dismiss Rowe from his position as mine Captain, although he resigned before they were able to do so. One allegation made at the time but not publicly proved was that Rowe had exchanged a turbine at the mine with a less powerful one which had been installed in the mill. From this date, it would appear that Rowe's personal financial situation worsened somewhat. Another consequence of his resignation was his removal to Douglas to live at Min Y Don, on Strathallan Crescent.

In November 1873 the plantation owned by Rowe to the rear of the Mill was found to be on fire. The undergrowth and trees were particularly dry and the fire quickly gained a hold. At the top of the plantation, gunpowder was stored in a secure compound for the Great Laxey Mining Company which it was feared would be threatened by the flames. A number of men armed with hatchets and saws broke away the side of the race supplying the mill allowing the water to run

down the hillside extinguishing the fire. Although on this occasion the building itself was not damaged, fire unfortunately would not be a stranger to the mill in future years.

On 23rd August, 1876 the *Mona's Herald* carried a notice advising that the Mill was to be offered for sale by auction on 6th September. It was stated that Rowe's sole reason for wishing to dispose of the property was that having taken up permanent resident in Douglas he was unable to give the personal attention to the mill business which it required. Given that operation of the mill was in the capable hands of Thomas Corlett and that Rowe had many other interests in Laxey, including his role as Member of the House of Keys for the area, this reason would seem to be unlikely. In reality, the mill was suffering financially, the competition from the importation of cheap English Flour now being very severe. Rowe's personal financial situation would also appear to have been declining. A wealth of fascinating information about the mill was revealed in the sale notice. There were now eight pairs of grinding stones with provision for two additional pairs should a future need arise. The installation of the steam engine was noted although the main source of power was still river-based and was

This view of Laxey, from Baldhoon, taken during the late 1890s, clearly shows the original constructional style of the roof of the mill.

Photo, collection Andrew Scarffe.

noted as having a head of water of 77 feet. Attached to the mill was a mechanic's shop which contained a lathe, forge and other tools; a dwelling house for the manager; two adjoining cottages for workmen; stabling for 12 horses and a piggery. Excluded from the sale were two warehouses, one at Ramsey used as a wholesale and retail store and the main warehouse at Laxey quay which was said to be capable of holding 20,000 bushels (a unit to measure dry volume) of grain. An option to lease these two buildings was available to the potential purchaser. Twenty-one acres of land surrounding the mill were included in the sale. It was also noted that *"the Isle of Man produces a very large quantity of grain annually and that, as the result of the extended and improved farming operations for which the Island is so justly celebrated, this production is still on the increase. The consequence of this and of the increasing prosperity of the Great Laxey Mine and other rising mines in the immediate neighbourhood, is that the local trade of the mill is steadily and largely augmenting"*. Despite the optimistic tone of the sale notice, no bids were made at the auction and the sale was withdrawn.

It was not until November 1879 that Rowe finally managed to sell the mill and, in the event, it was miller Thomas Corlett who was the purchaser. The sale was recorded in a deed dated 4th March 1880 in which it was revealed that the purchase price paid by Corlett was

One of the earliest known photographs of the mill, taken in the late 1890s, shows the original two storey screen house and the fine brick chimney to the rear of the mill. Two horse drawn carts loaded with sacks of grain stand outside the mill. The Glen Gardens Pavilion, which had been considerably enlarged in 1895, is visible to the right.

Photo, collection
John Kneale.

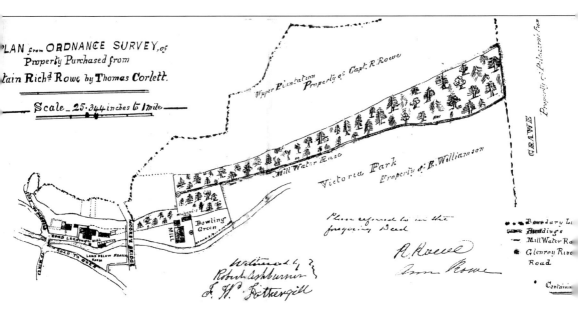

The plan of the land and buildings sold to Thomas Corlett by Richard Rowe accompanied the title deed of 1880.

£2,100. If the construction price of the mill as quoted in 1876 and the subsequent investment was indeed correct, then the venture could hardly have be described as a successful one for Rowe. Some indication of the probable complexities of Rowe's financial arrangements is revealed in two surviving letters dating to January, 1880. In the first, Thomas Corlett wrote to Rowe apologising for not being in a position to "settle the mill business"; Corlett blamed the terms imposed by Henry Bloom Noble (one of the Island's notable businessmen of the time) from whom it would appear Corlett had obtained a loan to purchase the mill. On the following day, Rowe wrote to his banker George Dumbell explaining that he had expected payment of £700 from Thomas Corlett and, from a source in London, "a considerable sum of money" which had not been forthcoming; Rowe promised to have his account in order shortly!

Shortly after the sale had been finalised, Thomas took his eldest son Thomas Stephen Corlett into partnership while his second son Robert Teare Corlett joined a year later; both were trained as millers. During the next few years the mill struggled to survive as the competition from imported flour was very severe.

During the last two decades of the nineteenth century, the British milling industry was transformed with the introduction of the "gradual reduction roller system". Traditional millstones ground grain in one operation; the various parts of the grain had to be separated out after grinding had taken place. Roller milling separated the constituents of the grain in a process called gradual reduction using a series of chilled iron rollers each of which performed a slightly different function on the grain, with a range of sifting and screening devices used to extract the flour. White flour produced by the roller method was of a superior quality and a greater quantity was obtained. British millers were increasingly purchasing wheat supplies from overseas particularly from America where the climate was more suited to its production. The imported wheat tended to be harder than British-grown wheat and the traditional millstones were not suited to processing it. This prompted a rapid introduction of the roller system throughout Britain. The British flour market was also being affected by the importation of flour from America and as the demand for whiter flour increased, mills faced a choice of trying to survive producing a lower grade product or investing in the roller system.

The roller milling system was pioneered by a Swiss engineer Henry Simon who had settled in Manchester in 1867. Simon built the first roller mill in Britain for McDougalls in Manchester in 1878 and his system revolutionised British milling. By 1887 it was reported that there were over 400 mills in Britain using the roller technology. During the same year, faced with the same problems of cheap imports of better graded flour, Thomas Corlett decided to install the roller system in the Laxey Glen Mill. The machinery was supplied by noted milling engineer, J Harrison Carter of Mark Lane in London. The new equipment was delivered to Laxey by the steamer Vulcan at the end of November, the *Mona's Herald* noting that the *"consignment consists of everything requisite for a complete automatic roller plant for the manufacture of wheat into flour"*. Inside the mill, the old grinding stones were removed but the turbine was retained to power the new machinery. Thomas Corlett was loathe to remove the old millstones in which he had taken great pride in dressing and maintaining but he had accepted that this was the only way that the mill would survive. The only other Manx mill to convert to the roller system was the Nunnery Mill situated on the outskirts of Douglas, which for a time was owned by the Corlett family.

An unusual incident occurred at the beginning of November, 1881 when four young men employed by the Great Laxey Mine were found guilty of willfully damaging the Laxey Glen Mill lade. A large rock had been rolled down through the plantation, crashing through the lade and causing damage which cost £2 15s to repair. Each was fined £1 and ordered to pay the repair cost or be imprisoned for one month.

Proposals to construct a steam railway between Douglas and Laxey had been made on a number of occasions since the mid 1870s and in December, 1882 one such scheme was laid before Tynwald for legislative approval. Although an increasing number of visitors were coming to Laxey during the summer months, it was the goods traffic, particularly in connection with the mine, which the promoters were keen to carry. A few horse-drawn carts plied daily between Douglas and Laxey carrying goods along the main road which was little more than a rough track. The journey by boat could be even more dangerous, especially in the winter months. As a consequence, the cost of carrying goods between the two places was high. Amongst those supporting the construction of the steam railway was Thomas Corlett who stated that the mill carted about 800 tons of wheat and flour between Douglas and Laxey each year. Most of the wheat used by the mill was of foreign origin and almost all of this was imported though Douglas harbour as Laxey was considered too dangerous and the principal market for the flour was in Douglas. The mill was capable of grinding nearly 4000 tons of wheat each year but the difficulty of cartage meant that the total actually milled was a lot less. Corlett believed he would have a much greater chance of competing with imported flour if the cartage cost was reduced. The mill was currently paying a cartage cost of 7s per ton and the cost of using the proposed railway was estimated at 2s per ton. Corlett revealed that Captain Rowe gave up the mill due to the competition from imported flour and that the cost of cartage was a major factor. Despite the support of many businesses and people in Laxey, the steam railway was not built and the village had to wait until 1894 for the electric tramway to be opened.

On 3rd February, 1910 Thomas Corlett died; his health had been failing for some time. After a service at Lonan Wesleyan Chapel, he was interred at Lonan Parish Churchyard. The Mill ownership passed to his two sons, Thomas and Robert. Thomas would also become an MHK for the sheading whilst Robert, who was a Justice of the Peace, became Captain of the Parish of Lonan. The business was restyled as "Thomas Corlett and Sons Ltd, Laxey and Douglas". In order to increase trade, premises known as "The Old Custom House" at 19 North Quay, Douglas was taken over from a Mr Beck.

Although some changes had been made to the mill during the intervening years, Thomas and Robert almost immediately began a remodelling of the machinery. Two extra floors were added to the screening

Subsequent to the death of Thomas Corlett Snr in 1910, the Mill was run by his son, R T Corlett, (top) along with his brother, Thomas. Both died shortly after the disastrous fire of 1922 and they were succeeded by Sidney (centre) and Neil Corlett (lower) who, along with Gilbert Corlett formed the new board of Thomas Corlett Ltd to run Laxey Glen Mill in 1923.

Photos, collection
John Kneale.

house to accommodate additional machinery and a connecting gangway to the main mill building was constructed. A 76HP suction gas engine supplied by Tangye Brothers of Birmingham and fuelled by anthracite, replaced the steam engine. New milling machinery was provided by Briddon and Fowler of Bredbury, Cheshire who were to be taken over by Henry Simon Ltd in 1915. The alterations were carried out by Gellings Foundry of Douglas and a plaque still survives in the mill recording their involvement.

A considerable quantity of flour was carried to Douglas on the Manx Electric Railway. In 1911 a scheme was proposed by the MER's engineer R J Newall to construct a branch line from the tramway to the mill. Commencing at a point to the rear of the present Isle of Man Bank building, the proposed line, of necessity steeply graded, would have passed beneath the main road viaduct, Moores Bridge and in a semi circle behind the mill to a point adjacent to the river. Nothing came of this scheme or a later proposal to construct an aerial ropeway between the mill and tram line.

From the turn of the century, the gradual decline in the Great Laxey Mine and a correspondingly diminished population had been offset by an increase in tourism which ensured a continued demand for flour. Following the outbreak of the First World War, the tourist trade all but vanished but the creation of a number of internment camps on the Island brought a vast number of

27

internees to the Island. At one time, Knockaloe Camp near Peel housed over 25,000 people. The provision of food for such huge numbers of people ensured that the demand for the mill's products was sustained through the war, the mill now being the principal supplier of flour on the Island. The Nunnery Mill at Douglas was taken over at this time for a short period to provide additional production capacity and storage.

In 1915, the mill purchased one of the very first steam wagons to be used on the Island. Built by Foden, the wagon was used to deliver products to the Douglas warehouse. However, the weight of the wagon damaged the surface of the main road between Douglas and Ramsey with the result that, as detailed in a later chapter, the Isle of Man Highway Board successfully sued the Mill in 1917 to recover the cost of repairs to the road. The wagon was sold to a Warrington-based firm in 1918. During the same year the company merged with the Ramsey business operated by Mr T B Cowley and was restyled as T Corlett and Sons & T B Cowley Ltd.

During February, 1918 electric lighting was installed in the mill, the power being sourced from a 9HP Gunther Francis turbine coupled directly to a 5 kilowatt dynamo running at 1000 revs per minute. The water supply was taken from the main mill lade and it is recalled that during the autumn months the lights in the mill would dip when leaves blocked the intake race.

1910 saw some significant alterations to the mill and to the way the business was operated. The illustration clearly shows the additional two floors which were added to the screen room on the left hand side of the mill.

Photo, collection John Kneale.

With prices of foodstuffs falling and large stocks of flour in hand, milling temporarily ceased at the beginning of November 1920 while a complete overhaul of the milling machinery which had been used almost continuously during the war was carried out. On the morning of 5th January 1921, milling resumed; only ten hours later the mill would be almost totally destroyed by one the worst fires ever experienced in Laxey. Shortly after 12.30 pm an outbreak of fire was discovered on the ground floor of the mill. Within minutes flames had engulfed almost the entire building spreading through the wooden grain chutes which connected the floors. Thirty men were at work and all had to run from the building through the fire escapes. The mill had its own internal fire hydrants and hoses fed from the mill cistern and lade and a brave attempt was made by the men to fight the fire but the heat was so intense that the hoses were quickly abandoned. The Laxey Fire Brigade, formed only a few months earlier, was quickly on the scene but with limited equipment consisting of little more than a hand cart and a few hoses, and totally reliant on the water pressure from the hydrants connected to the village water system, their efforts were ineffective. By this time the flames had reached the roof which was quickly engulfed and came crashing down inside the building sending flames higher than the tall chimney at the rear. At 1.00 pm, assistance was requested from the Douglas Fire Brigade. Two members of the brigade commandeered a car from the Athol Garage and, loaded with hose and pipes, set off for Laxey where they arrived twenty minutes later. It was realized that nothing could be done to save the main mill building and the firemen turned their attention to save the adjacent screening house, the roof of which was now beginning to burn. Meanwhile at Douglas, two horses were obtained to haul the fire engine which, with six fire men on board, set off for Laxey at 1.10 pm. It took over one and a half hours for the brigade to arrive at the Mill by which time the building had been almost totally destroyed with just the four stone walls still left standing. The *Isle of Man Weekly Times* recorded that *"the horses were covered in perspiration and looked thoroughly worn out long before they arrived on the scene. When the engine did arrive at Laxey the crowd gave a hearty cheer but by that time there was practically nothing left of the mill"*. A further twenty minutes were to pass before the engine had raised sufficient steam to operate the suction pumps although another ten minutes elapsed before they could be induced to work. The fire engine was then moved to the rear of the building and the fire was prevented from spreading to the adjacent engine house. The efforts of the Douglas Fire Brigade had saved the screen house. It was assumed

that the fire had been started by a breakage of machinery causing friction sparks to ignite flour dust which had quickly spread to the wooden grain chutes and silk sieves. It was estimated that the damage to the mill was £60,000 of which only £20,000 was insured. The mill had the unfortunate distinction of being the biggest loss due to fire in the Isle of Man to that date. A new supply of wheat valued at £5000 had been placed in the mill the previous day and was also destroyed. The Douglas Brigade stood down in the evening but the Laxey

The 1921 fire swept through the building which was almost destroyed. The lower scene was from the Glen Gardens, behind the mill.

Photos, collection John Kneale.

Brigade stayed in attendance overnight to dampen down the smouldering remains.

Although English mills had managed to regain some of the Manx flour market, the Island was still largely dependent on supplies from the Laxey Mill. Emergency plans were put in place by the mill to obtain flour from English suppliers and the first cargo arrived at Ramsey within several days of the fire.

During the following week, the weather turned stormy and it was feared that the strong winds would blow down the walls but they had been extremely well built and stood firm. The insurance assessor stipulated that men be kept on constant standby with hoses for a week to dampen down the smouldering remains. In the event it was over three weeks before they were allowed to stand down. A number of the former workers at the mill were able to find employment clearing away the debris. Four weeks later smoke was still coming from the smouldering timbers as they were cleared away. Unfortunately, there was criticism of the Douglas Brigade, particularly about the time they had taken to reach the fire and the problems experienced with their equipment, which led to comments being made at a meeting of the Town Council. It was, perhaps, overlooked that the Douglas Brigade had attended the fire which was out of the Douglas area and that the Laxey Brigade's efforts had proved futile due to their lack of equipment.

The destruction of the flour mill could not have occurred at a worse time for Laxey. The Great Laxey Mine had closed in May 1920; it was feared at the time that this closure would be permanent. Many men in the village were unemployed and now an additional thirty men also found themselves without work.

There were other victims of the fire too. Later in the year Robert Teare Corlett died at the age of 59. The health of his elder brother, Thomas Stephen Corlett, deteriorated and he died on 11th January, 1922. It was assumed that the health of both men had suffered from the shock of seeing the mill destroyed.

During May 1922, Laxey businessman and philanthropist Robert Williamson re-opened the Great Laxey Mine, much to the relief of the nearly one hundred Laxey men who were unemployed. However, the mill still remained derelict. This was to change during November 1923 when it was somewhat unexpectedly announced that Laxey Glen Mill was to be rebuilt and re-opened. A restructuring of Thos Corlett and Sons & T B Cowley Ltd from the 1st December saw the formation of two subsidiary companies. Corlett, Sons and Cowley Ltd took over the seed and corn businesses located in Douglas and Ramsey under the directorship of Thomas Cowley, Sidney Corlett and Hubert Corlett while the other company, Thomas Corlett Ltd, assumed the responsibility of the Laxey Glen Mill, under the directorship of Neil Corlett, Gilbert Corlett and Sidney Corlett.

Rebuilding of the mill was carried out by Messrs J D Kelly and Sons of Kirk Michael and work commenced during the middle week of November clearing away the remaining debris on the site. At the beginning of January 1924, the large brick chimney at the rear of the mill which once served the auxiliary steam engine was demolished, although this took several attempts. Ropes were tied around the chimney and attached to a traction engine; the attempt to pull it down failed. A second attempt using explosives was equally unsuccessful. For the third attempt, bricks were removed from the structure on the side facing away from the mill and dynamite charges were set off in the interior, the chimney falling onto the flat ground to the rear of the mill. Progress on the rebuilding of the mill was rapid, the stone walls fortunately being almost undamaged. New floors of polished maple wood were installed on steel girders which replaced the wooden floor beams of the old mill. At the beginning of February 1924, the new roof had been completed and rebuilt as a single span on a steel framework, replacing the earlier double span. By the end of the month, reconstruction of the building was almost complete with just the new windows remaining to be installed. At the same time, a contract was placed with the now world-renowned firm of milling engineers Messrs Henry Simon Ltd of Manchester for the new milling machinery. On 29th August, 1924 the *Isle of Man Examiner* was able to report that the reconstruction of the mill was complete and production had started although there some minor problems with the machinery. By the middle of September it as reported that the mill was now in full working order and a large quantity of flour was being produced. There were nearly forty men employed and orders were such that the men were working overtime.

An official re-opening ceremony was held at the beginning of October when sixty bakers and wholesalers were given a conducted tour of the reconstructed mill and the new machinery by Messrs Swales and Whittaker who supervised the installation on behalf of Henry Simon Ltd. Neil Corlett had supervised much of the reconstruction work on behalf of the mill.

Known as the "Alphega-Plansifter" system, it was typical of milling machinery being installed by Henry Simon Ltd in what were termed

A group of workers pose for the photographer outside the main entrance to the mill. Taken sometime prior to the 1921 fire, the photograph clearly shows the original style of the windows. Note also the cobblestones in front of the platform.

Photo collection, Andrew Scarffe.

"small country mills". At Laxey, the machinery was arranged so that the capacity of the mill could be doubled without requiring an extension of the building. In its publicity, a great emphasis was placed on the fact that the products were not touched by "human hand" throughout the milling process, which was summarised in the *Isle of Man Examiner*. The newspaper report gave an interesting summary of the new milling process:

Most of the wheat was imported into Laxey harbour on small coastal steamers, approximately 200 tons at a time, bagged in 25 cwt sacks. Initially stored in the warehouse on the quayside, the sacks of wheat were then taken by the Foden steam wagon to the mill where it was either stored in a shed adjacent to the road bridge or tipped directly into the hopper of the main intake elevator. After receiving a preliminary cleaning, the wheat was then delivered to four "dirty wheat" bins each of which had a capacity of 300 sacks. During the reconstruction of the mill, the existing wheat cleaning machines were overhauled and a number of new machines installed. The wheat was also passed over a series of magnets which removed any metallic items; this also prevented any pieces of scrap from damaging the milling rollers. It was noted that pieces of rust from the hulls of the coastal steamers often found its way into the wheat. After dry cleaning and a series of con-

33

ditioning processes, the wheat passed over a Simon "emery scourer" before going to the first break rolls. There were two rows of the latest type Simon rollers for carrying out the reduction process. These were fitted with 'Alphega' separators, the stock from these and the first reductions were lifted to the top floor of the building to six Simon 'free swinging sifters', then either to Simon 'fan less purifiers' or to centrifugal dressing machines installed on the same floor. The wheat passed through twelve separate processes before the bran and inner skins were removed and the fine flour treated and graded.

Between the various processes, the products were carried in close-jointed wooden chutes made from polished yellow pine. The flour was carried by means of worm conveyors to the packers and the filled sacks were then trucked to the warehouse where there were three floors for storage." It was noted that a "spotless shining cleanliness pervades the whole of the mill with an entire absence of dust usually associated with the craft of milling".

Power to operate the machinery was taken from a "Girrard" turbine developing up to 60 hp; presumably this replaced the earlier turbine as part of the rebuilding process. The auxiliary power system continued to be worked by the 76 hp Tangye suction gas plant which was used when there was insufficient water to drive the turbine, usually for about three months during each summer. Electric lighting and heating was powered from a 9 hp Gunther Francis turbine coupled directly to a 5 kilowatt dynamo running at 1000 rpm; this may have been the original 1918 installation which had survived undamaged by the fire. At this time, the mill could produce three grades of flour and had an output of three 280 lb sacks of flour per hour. This equated to

This photograph, dating to the mid 1930s, shows a number of the original mill stones resting against the mill frontage. The banks of the adjacent Laxey River had been reconstructed following a disastrous flood in 1930.

Photo collection, Andrew Scarffe.

34

a maximum output of 300 sacks per week which accounted for half of the Island's total flour requirement of 600 sacks per week.

As the decade passed, the air of optimism evident following the rebuilding of the mill lessened somewhat. Although at the beginning of 1926, semolina was added to the range of products, during the autumn of the same year production ceased entirely due to a wide-spread depression in the flour market but also partly due to the nation-wide miners' strike which affected the import of wheat stocks. It was not until the end of February 1927 before the mill re-opened.

Shortly after midday on 25th August 1928, fire broke out on the third floor of the mill. Using the internal hoses and hydrants, a group of workers under the direction of the mill manager were able to extinguish the blaze. Unfortunately an hour later the fire broke out again. Travelling up the wooden grain shutes, the flames quickly set fire to the roof timbers. Laxey Fire Brigade were called and arrived at the mill within minutes and managed to prevent the flames spreading further. Douglas Fire Brigade arrived an hour later having been delayed en route at Onchan while a broken spring on the fire engine was repaired. As a crowd of several hundred onlookers watched from the road bridge, tiles were removed from the roof by the firemen so that they could gain access to the blaze inside, which took a further two hours to be extinguished. However, in the early hours of Sunday morning the fire again broke out and was again extinguished by the Laxey Fire Brigade with the assistance of four Douglas firemen who had made their way to Laxey in a borrowed car. It was assumed that the fire had been started by a piece of metal which had found its way into the machinery causing friction sparks and igniting the dry flour dust. The damage was estimated at over £2000 although it is not clear what period of time elapsed before repairs were completed.

In 1932 Gilbert Corlett, son of Robert Teare Corlett and grandson of Thomas Corlett opened a small Tattersall mill on Ramsey quayside known as the Eureka Mills. He was joined by his brother Norman who had served an apprenticeship at the Hereford Flour Mills before returning to Laxey Glen Mill in 1924. The brothers had operated a provender business together for a few years in Tower Street, Ramsey until in December, 1929 Norman left the Island for three years to manage a mill in Kenya. The business proved successful which encouraged Gilbert to acquire the Laxey Glen Mill from the restructured Messrs Corlett & Sons and T B Cowley Ltd and form a new company Messrs R G Corlett Ltd to operate the mill. However, some sources record that Gilbert had moved back to Laxey and resumed

milling there in 1932. In 1935, Norman was appointed as mill manager. A flaked maize plant was installed.

In 1939, with the world again plunged into war, perhaps now for the first time the true value of the mill to the Island was readily appreciated. As had occurred during the First World War, tourism temporarily collapsed and internment camps were established across the Island. Once again the mill worked day and night to provide flour to meet the needs of the local population, the internees and members of the armed forces stationed on the Island. In a generous and patriotic gesture, Gilbert Corlett approached the Island's governor and proposed that he be paid a salary by the government for the duration of the war in return for which the government would retain all the profits made from milling - £106,960 was paid over to the government during this period. This arrangement continued for a couple of years after the war until further modernisation of the machinery was required and

Sales Manager, Fred Baxendale, white overall standing, with a number of the staff of the Mill in an undated photograph thought to be around 1949.

Photo collection
Mike Kelly.

the mill directors approached the governor to be released from the arrangement. During the war, some alterations and additions had taken place to the mill outbuildings including a new office, new sheds and a new grain store. All were built by Laxey builder Edwin C Kneale, who some years earlier in 1937 had saved the Laxey Wheel from almost certain demolition.

On Monday 13th May, 1946 for the third time in twenty five years, the mill was badly damaged by another outbreak of fire. Shortly after 2.30 pm, a fire was discovered in the engine room. With a wet sack pulled over his head, Norman Corlett ran into the engine room through the thick black diesel smoke and was able to switch off the engine. Almost suffocated by the smoke, he fought the flames with fire extinguishers but unfortunately, just as the fire was almost extinguished he was forced from the building. Within five minutes, the Laxey Fire Brigade had arrived and found that the flames had rapidly moved up the building through the elevator shafts to the top floor. The firemen attempted to extinguish the blaze by pouring water down the shafts before they too were driven from the building by the smoke and heat and had to concentrate on fighting the fire from outside. Clouds of dense smoke caused by burning diesel in the engine poured from the windows and roof of the building. Douglas Fire Brigade arrived and built a temporary dam across the adjacent river and pumped water onto the flames. Just when the combined efforts of the two brigades were controlling the fire, the roof collapsed inside the building fueling the fire with flames reaching over twenty feet into the air above the building. By 5.30 pm, the fire had finally been extinguished but the two top floors of the building were almost destroyed and over one hundred tons of flour and the remnants of a cargo of grain stored in the building were ruined. At the time the mill had been increasing its production to cope with the anticipated demand at the start of the first post war tourist season. The fire was caused by diesel dripping from a fractured fuel pipe onto the hot exhaust pipe of the engine and then spreading along the dusty canvas drive belt.

During the fire, as the Douglas Fire Brigade was pumping water from the temporary dam, the river below the mill almost completely dried out. A Laxey resident recalls as a child trying to catch trout from the remaining pools of water as the firemen, a few yards further up the river, battled to save the mill!

Salvage work began the next day and a temporary galvanised roof was built across the top floor. With the able assistance of builder Edwin Kneale and the supervision of the mill's management, partial

On fire again! May 1946 brought the third serous fire in 25 years. Douglas Fire Brigade's 30HP Fordson fire engine EMN 823 is in attendance.

Photo collection,
Andrew Scarffe

production began only 21 days later. During the following year, mains electricity was supplied to the mill.

At approximately this time (and possibly as a result of the fire), the animal feed operation was relocated into the Manx Electric Railway's former power station on the Glen Road. This arrangement lasted for a few years before relocation back to the mill.

A considerable portion of the machinery had been damaged in the fire. Whereas previously the mill had operated two nine hour shifts, from 6.00am to 3.00pm and from 3.00pm to midnight, it was now necessary to work the remaining machinery continuously in order to produce the same volume of flour, a situation which practicably could not be allowed to continue for any lengthy period of time. In February, 1949 work began on the remodeling of the mill with new machinery being supplied and installed by Henry Simon Ltd of Manchester. The installation work was cleverly carried out to allow milling to continue throughout the rebuilding process. One notable feature was the myriad of wooden chutes made on site by Henry

Simon's joiners; it was recalled that teams of joiners worked from tool benches set up on each floor. Power was taken from a Mirlees diesel engine operating a generator, thus making the mill one of the most modern at the time; further alterations were to take place to the power equipment in 1951. A sprinkler system was installed by Mather and Platt Ltd of Manchester who during the 1890s had supplied much of the pioneering electrical equipment during the construction of the Manx Electric Railway.

Installation of the new machinery was completed at the beginning of June and there were now 27 permanent staff employed. Then, only a few days later on the 18th of June, Gilbert Corlett died suddenly at his home, Ellerslie Farm, Marown; he was 47 years of age. His widow, Mrs Ruth Corlett was appointed as chairman of the company and Norman Corlett was now appointed company manager. Former employees recalled that Gilbert was a firm but very fair employer. Sadly, Neil Corlett had died the previous year

In 1950 a laboratory was added to the mill's facilities. Quality checks which were becoming more and more important with each harvest could now be carried out at the mill rather than having to send samples of wheat to the United Kingdom for testing. It also enabled some financial savings to be made.

In 1955 two changes were made which enabled wheat to be imported as loose cargoes rather than in sacks as had been the case since the mill opened. Edwin Kneale constructed a new three section storage silo at the rear of the mill capable of holding 700 tons of loose wheat. At the same time a mobile semi-pneumatic suction machine was purchased from a company called "Grainveyor". Labour troubles at Liverpool docks had resulted in loose wheat being imported which then had to be filled into sacks to unload the boat, a long and laborious process. The Grainveyor could be towed behind a wagon to the harbour where it sucked the loose wheat from the cargo holds directly into a five ton capacity metal box placed on the back of tipper lorries. In 1960, 32 ships brought nearly 6000 tons of grain to the Island with 18 unloading at Ramsey and the remainder at Laxey. For many years until the late 1970s wagons belonging to local haulage contractor Edgar Kinrade were used to transport the wheat from the harbours to the mill. However, for the children of Laxey there was an unfortunate side effect when the cargoes changed from sacked wheat to loose wheat. Previously, in a ritual which would be impossible to imagine in today's Health and Safety conscious society, word would quickly pass around the Laxey children when a grain boat had berthed at the harbour. As a treat the children were allowed to travel on the wagons as they ran up

The mill rolls, originally installed by Henry Simon in 1924 in situ on the first floor of the mill. The square, wooden flour transfer chutes which fed them are clearly identifiable.

and down to the harbour, either on the empty wagon or perched aloft on the grain sacks!

During autumn 1956, Edwin Kneale began the construction of a three floor extension to the main building which would provide additional warehouse to store sacks of flour. Constructed on a steel frame on the side of the building adjacent to the river and straddling the access road at the side leading to the rear of the mill, the front elevation was built with stonework to exactly match the height and style of the original mill building, while the side and rear were clad with asbestos sheeting. Only when viewed from the side or rear of the mill is it apparent that this portion is actually an extension. The extension was designed by Douglas-based architect T Kennaugh and the stonework was constructed by stonemason Wilfie Kermode. An internal spiral chute was constructed in the mill down which sacks of flour could be dropped to the delivery wagons waiting below. Around the same time a Sizer Cubing Plant was installed to produce cubes and pellets of animal feed. Having proved successful, the plant was later enlarged.

During 1955, Mr Bill Richardson was appointed as miller. Born in Dublin, he served a milling apprenticeship with the Dock Milling

The Mill's leading brand - Sunrise - as it was marketed in the '60s.

Company. He then moved to India where he served as manager of the Reform Flour Mills in Calcutta for ten years before moving on to Pakistan and ultimately to Laxey. Assistant manager and transport controller at the time was Mr Fred Baxendale who had joined R G Corlett Ltd in 1935.

In 1960 the Mill celebrated its centenary. A special celebratory supplement was issued by the *Isle of Man Examiner* which reported that confectionary flour with brand names *Manx Queen, Manx King, Manx Pioneer* and *Flavo* were supplied in bulk to bakers and *Pioneer, Sunrise* and *Flavo* flours were sold in retail outlets. There were thirty-six other varieties of animal and poultry feeds made by the mill. At this time the Board of Directors consisted of Chairman Mrs Ruth Corlett, Manager Mr Norman Corlett and Company Secretary Mr John Bolton who was also the Member of the House of Keys for West Douglas; he had been appointed in 1950. A celebratory centenary dinner was held at the Laxey Glen Hotel.

Visibly, business continued as usual during the next few years. In 1963 an old shed used for storage of bagged wheat was demolished and in 1968 a further extension was constructed by the Ramsey Shipyard at the rear of the mill to house new flour mixing machinery and storage bins for wheatings. A 33 inch diameter clock was installed on the front of the building by G and R Ridgway Ltd in August 1970. However, the financial situation of the company was now beginning

The "Grainveyor" was bought to unload loose grain from the holds of the ships berthing at Laxey and Ramsey harbours. In this picture taken on Laxey harbour side, grain is being loaded into a metal box fitted to the back of Edgar Kinrade's Bedford lorry FMN 555.

Photo collection, Andrew Scarffe.

The 1960 management team - Bill Richardson, Miller (right), and Fred Baxendale, assistant Manager and Transport Controller.

to decline. The cost of imported wheat was relentlessly increasing and attempts to increase the cost of flour were met with resistance from bakers who were also criticised when they attempted to increase the price of bread. Any such price increases had to be carefully balanced against the threat of imported flour and bread to the local markets. The animal feed operations were also suffering a financial decline as the cost of raw materials and additives were increasing and breakdowns of the machinery were becoming more frequent.

On 1st January 1973, the United Kingdom joined the European Community and agreed to adopt the Common Agricultural Policy. In short, by imposing levies on the import of grain from outside the EEC and the fixing of minimum producers prices, the cost of

R. G. Corlett Ltd. board at the time of the Mill's centenary was Mrs Ruth Corlett, Chairman, Mr Norman Corlett, Manager and Mr J. B. Bolton MHK (left) who was Company Secretary.

Canadian wheat was soon to increase even further. An additional cost was incurred from 1st April 1973 when Laxey harbour was closed to commercial traffic and all wheat cargoes had to be transported by road either from Ramsey or Douglas.

By the early 1970s, certain members of the Isle of Man Government were becoming increasing concerned about the possible closure of the mill. From the late 1960s, the mill had been obliged to maintain a three month stock of wheat on behalf of the government as part of a strategic food reserve and there was an equal concern about the loss of employment and the addition of another 40 skilled and semi-skilled operatives to the Island's unemployment register.

Towards the end of 1973, the directors of R G Corlett Ltd gave notice to the Isle of Man Government of their intention to cease trading. During December, the government finally took some action. As the mill was having difficulty meeting payment of its latest consignment of Canadian wheat, the government agreed to release supplies of wheat and made arrangements with the Isle of Man Bank for overdraft facilities for the Company, to ease cash flow problems and enable payment for wheat cargoes.

At the January 1974 sitting of Tynwald, Speaker of the House of Keys, Charles Kerruish, stated that the mill should be nationalized and successfully moved that a Select Committee of five members should be appointed to consider the terms by which the government would acquire the undertaking and assets of the mill business, to ensure for the Manx People the maintenance of an acceptable level of flour and bread supplies. A grant of £11,000 was made to the mill to enable a purchase of Canadian wheat and a further £9,900 was given during February for the same purpose; a cargo of wheat was awaiting shipment at Liverpool but the suppliers were not prepared to deliver unless a guarantee of payment was made. Industrial unrest in the United Kingdom was also causing the government some concern and it was feared that wheat deliveries could temporarily cease. Representatives of two English companies had visited the mill but both had been dissuaded from purchase by the potential investment required on capital improvements and by the limited Manx market for the products.

A few weeks later, the Tynwald Select Committee under the chairmanship of Percy Radcliffe, Chairman of the Finance Board, recommended that the government should nationalise the mill, a decision which was endorsed by the government's Executive Council. On 13th May, Government took over the running of R G Corlett Ltd. It was a historic decision when, on 9th July 1974, Tynwald supported the

The official centenary photograph of the Mill staff and management. Back Row; left to right - Freddie Kermode, Harry Kermeen, Roy Kermode, Russell Henry, Leslie Corlett, Norman Kneale, Albert Fleming, Jimmy Cowley, Steve Skillicorn, John Kneale. Third Row; left to right - Jack Haddock, Alan Bridson, John Gorry, Jim Moughtin, Joe Brown, Bernard Cowley, Norman Kewley, Gilbert Collister, John Clague. Second Row; left to right - Mattie Quine, Bert Moughtin, Freddie Lawton, Eric Caley, Colin Towers, Robert Clague, Tommy Kissack, Jim Bridson, Alfie Ball, Willie Clague. Front Row; left to right - Sid Kinnish, Edward Godfrey, Bill Richardson (Managing Director), Norman Corlett (Chairman), Freddie Baxendale (Sales Manager) Jane Long (nee Quirk), Stevie Lace. . Photo Collection, John Kneale.

45

Executive Council's decision and Mr Radcliffe's motion recommending nationalisation for a purchase price of £65,000. Tynwald recognised that it was the only flour mill still in operation on the Island and that it was strategically necessary to retain flour making capabilities; memories of wartime shortages and the 1966 national seaman's strike when the Island was without scheduled shipping services were recalled. Additionally, the Mill gave valuable employment in Laxey to nearly forty people. The deal included the mill property and equipment including grain drying machinery, seven vehicles and the dwellings known as Mill House and Mill Cottage. It also gave Tynwald the right to trade as Laxey Glen Flour Mills and to use the propriety brand names for the products. Mr Radcliffe told Tynwald that the Mill would never be profitable again.

Loose grain was latterly imported for the Mill on the Ramsey Steamship Company's "Ben Veg" seen here docked at Laxey harbour which closed to all commercial traffic on 1st April, 1973.

Photo, Stan Basnett.

— 3 —

GOVERNMENT OWNERSHIP

O wnership of the nationalised mill was vested in Laxey Glen Mills Ltd, a private company limited by shares but wholly owned by the Isle of Man Government, and which initially had a share capital of £125,000 although this would be increased on a number of occasions during subsequent years. Laxey Glen Mills Ltd was incorporated on 11th July 1974 and its first directors were Mr W Alex Crowe, FCA who was appointed chairman; Mr John Corlett JP, a Lonan farmer and Bill Richardson, the mill's manager. Day to day operations continued largely unchanged from the immediate pre-nationalisation days. September, 1974 saw the retirement of Fred Baxendale who had built up a wide customer base and was a popular and enthusiastic member of the company. In September 1975, Mr Peter Duncan joined the board and later in the same month the membership was extended further through the appointment of Mr A J Winckle, a master baker from Foxdale. Production of soda bread flour began in 1975 and the first batch was exported to Northern Ireland during November.

For some time, the cost of Manx bread had been causing disquiet amongst local consumers and this was to escalate during 1976 when a supermarket considered importing cheap alternative brands. The Master Bakers Association, which represented the majority of bakers and

Mr Peter Duncan joined the Board in 1975 later taking over the Chairmanship in 1978

47

confectioners on the Island, demanded that the government completely ban any such imports. They were supported by the National Union of Farmers and the Mill from which the Association had at that time agreed to purchase all its flour. Importation of cheap bread obviously had the potential to cause great harm not only to the local bakers but also to the Mill. With the price of flour produced at Laxey being some fifteen per cent dearer than in the United Kingdom, the issue would be a recurring one throughout the next few years. Tynwald agreed during July to increase the share capital of the company to £300,000 with £200,000 shares being issued, to enable the purchase of additional machinery to improve and expand the animal feed production. Interestingly, the Tynwald debate which dealt with this issue included a number of speeches by members who were highly critical of Government taking over the company in 1974 but who now sought to congratulate the directors of the new company.

In response to the concerns over cheap bread, the government appointed a "Flour and Bread Commission" to investigate the pricing structure of the products. The directors of the mill in a letter to the committee expressed their great concern over the uncontrolled import of bread. The Committee's report, issued in January 1977, concluded that the price differential was acceptable as it was in the Island's interest to maintain milling operations, although there was no recommendation to ban imported breads. Some deficiencies in the operation of the mill were noted. This did not, however, pacify local consumers and suppliers and there were further attempts to import cheap bread later in the year. There was a vociferous reaction from the mill and the Island's bakers, the latter threatening to picket ships bringing the bread to the Island. The Ramsey Steamship Company also expressed concern as their vessel, *Ben Veg*, was used almost exclusively to carry wheat from Seaforth Dock to the Island for the mill and there were fears over the future employment of the vessel and its crew.

Exceptional rises in the cost of raw materials were blamed for a loss of £27,834 recorded at the end of the 1977 financial year; the previous year had seen a profit of £57,149. Unfortunately this coincided with a rise in the price of Manx bread which was now the dearest in the British Isles. The mill's claims that the two matters were not linked was greeted with little enthusiasm especially as the price of flour had again been increased only a few weeks earlier.

Discontent over the cost of locally produced bread rumbled on through 1978 and into 1979 when a plan to import bread in road containers and then distribute it to local supermarkets in a fleet of vans

permanently based on the Island became public knowledge. At the beginning of the same year, the "Bread Prices Commission" presented its report. The Commission had been appointed by Tynwald in 1978 to carry out a further investigation into all aspects of bread prices on the Island. The Commission concluded that the price of bread should not be reduced and that there should not be any control over the retail price. It was noted that the cost of local flour was greater than elsewhere in the United Kingdom as a direct result of the policy to retain milling at Laxey. It was recommended that the government subsidy on flour produced at the mill should continue, although the method of calculation should be amended. A major factor in the greater cost of flour when compared to the United Kingdom was the cost of shipping wheat to the Island, the associated unloading costs at the harbours and the cost of transportation to the mill. Flour was still delivered to all consumers in sacks and it was recommended that the purchase of a suitable vehicle to deliver flour in bulk should be considered. If the proposed vehicle was also suitable for carrying, further reductions in transportation costs should be possible. Some deficiencies in the operation of the mill were recorded and it was also noted that the location and size of the mill were not ideal. It was recommended that further investigation should be made into promoting wheat production on the Island. As a result, during the summer, a "wheat committee" was formed consisting of representatives from the Board of Agriculture, National Farmers Union and the Mill to encourage local farmers to grow more milling wheat but in the short

Bill Richardson retired from the Mill in 1984 and a party was held in his honour at the Glen Hotel, Laxey.

term this was not successful. Ill health had prompted the retirement of Chairman Crowe in February 1978, and his successor was Mr Duncan.

Chairman of the Government's Finance Board Mr Percy Radcliffe successfully sought another cash injection of £100,000 from Tynwald during October 1979 to further increase the share capital of the Company. It was reported to Tynwald that this was as a direct result of inflation and a heavier than expected capital requirement in buildings, plant and machinery. Although the resolution was approved, several members expressed their doubts about the Mill's future viability. The cash injection unfortunately coincided with another rise in the price of bread; a large sliced white loaf now cost 37p and it was forecast that the 40p loaf was not that far into the future.

Agreement was reached with Corlett Sons and Cowley Ltd to take over all deliveries of the Mill's animal foods to farmers with effect from 1st February 1980. The experiment, which it was hoped would result in more efficient deliveries, proved to be unsuccessful and was abandoned at the end of September.

1981 was an eventful year; during late April and early May Messrs Duncan, Corlett and Winckle all resigned as a result of a disagreement with the Managing Director. It was publicly reported that there had been a disagreement with government concerning the future operating policy for the mill and in particular the production of the animal foodstuffs which was incurring an annual loss. Government were forced to appoint a new board and Dr Edgar Mann MHK, Chairman of the Board of Agriculture and Fisheries, and Mr Noel Cringle MHK were appointed as directors, to join Mr Richardson who was the sole survivor from the previous board. It was evidently felt by Government that political appointees were required. However, Dr Mann, who in addition to his legislative responsibilities was the village doctor, resigned in December 1981 following appointment to the Board of Finance as it was felt that there was a potential conflict of interest. As a result Noel Cringle was appointed Chairman and Mr J Radcliffe and Mr Denis Tooley joined the Board, the latter having many years experience in the milling industry. The resignation of the previous Board was the first public indication that the animal foodstuff deficit was causing concern in some government circles. In 1982 it was recorded that the cost of retaining the Strategic Food Reserve was £68,995. That requirement still exists and the Mill conforms to the directive. Although the cost of retention is substantially larger, the direct cost to Government still remains much the same.

A demand by Manx bakers during 1982 for a complete ban on cheap bread imports was again rejected by Government which promised instead a further inquiry into what was termed the "crisis in the Manx bakery industry". The advent of roll on-roll off ferry services to the Island had made it easier for importers to bring in the bread. One supermarket was reported to be giving away free bread with petrol purchases. At the end of the year, Quirks Bakery in Douglas which had been producing bread for 102 years ceased trading. Despite such news controls on bread imports remained elusive.

In October, 1984 Tynwald voted an additional £20,000 to meet increased operating losses

David Corlett, Richardson's successor as Manager and Miller, Derek Osborn.

above the £90,000 already projected during the financial year. Increases in the price of Canadian wheat and competition from other local suppliers of animal foods were blamed. Tynwald approved the extra cash injection despite some concern over the increasing operating losses, but the value of the Mill to the Island was still appreciated. Members of Tynwald were told that it was clear that the Mill would never make a profit.

Bill Richardson suffered with health problems at the end of 1984 and, to ensure continuity of operations, Derek Osborn was asked by Noel Cringle to superintend milling operations during December. He was appointed as miller in January 1985 and brought with him over twenty years' milling experience, latterly with Spillers at Birkenhead. Bill Richardson retired during April after a career spent entirely in the milling industry and with thirty years service at Laxey. His successor was David Corlett who was descended from a Manx farming background and had returned to the Island after working in Nigeria. Although not related to the original Corlett family, it was pleasing to see the name once again associated with the Mill.

Mill workers demonstrate outside Tynwald in 1985 against the import of cheap bread. MHK Dominic Delaney appears to have some sympathy!

Controversy over the price of Manx bread was re-ignited in 1985 when businessman John Grocutt imported substantial quantities of Sunblest bread. Workers from the mill, concerned about the threat to their jobs, picketed Tynwald. Although the venture was short lived and Mr Grocutt subsequently left the Island, the episode resulted in a Commission of Enquiry, the "Baking Industry and Staple Commodities Commission" being set up by Government. Part of its remit included an assessment of current and future operations of the Mill. Evidence was taken from a number of interested parties including Ramsey Bakery which was now the principal user of the flour produced by the Mill. Further public support was offered by the National Farmers Union and the Transport and General Workers Union which represented the majority of the Mill employees. Government financial estimates for the year showed the Mill to be in receipt of a grant of £150,000 with an additional subsidy of £50,000; Government also met loan charges of £30,100. There was criticism from within Tynwald of the level of deficit but it was pointed out that the Mill paid the levy applied by the EEC on imports of Canadian wheat and that the amount paid back to the government through the levy that year was £189,989. The Commission's findings were duly presented to the government's Executive Council and it was expected that these would be made public by September 1987.

However, some of the conclusions of the report caused considerable concern within government circles and once again the deficit on the loss making animal foodstuff operation was highlighted. On 1st March 1987, the directors and management of the mill were sum-

moned to meet the Chief Minister (the ministerial system of govern-ment had by now replaced the earlier Boards) and representatives from the Department of Agriculture and the Treasury. To the aston-ishment of the Mill directors and manager, the Chief Minister announced that the decision had been taken to completely close Laxey Glen Mill on 30 September 1987 due to the continuing losses. However, after considerable protest by the directors, the closure date was later withdrawn.

The directors argued that the new management had made consider-able effort to increase efficiency. Accountancy methods had been mod-ernised, the animal feedstock formulation computerised and sales of animal foodstuff had improved. An additional feed store had been con-structed in 1986 giving additional storage space which permitted longer, and therefore more economical, production runs. A forklift truck had been purchased to avoid manual handling of sacks and bulk deliveries of feedstuffs were now being made to some farmers. Discussions had been made with mainland suppliers and local farmers to improve the formulation of the feeds. The directors were of the opinion that the feedstuff manufacturing could be kept in active operation until the turn of the century; with further investment they were certain this could be made profitable. Manx bakers had successfully been persuaded to reduce the volume of English flour used and flour sales were profitable. The directors further argued that machinery in the mill which should have been replaced was kept in operation on "a make and mend policy" due to an absence of funding. At the very least a partial refurbishment

His Excellency Laurence New with Mrs New, paid a vist to the Mill in May 1986. They were welcomed by Chairman Noel Cringle MHK who introduced Chairman of the Laxey Commissioners Mr Bill Kneale. Miller Derek Osborn stands left.

of the mill should be carried out. Production was increasing whilst the number of staff employed had been reduced through natural wastage.

Tynwald debated the Commission's report during December 1987 and after a three hour session it was agreed that Government would provide funding of £450,000 to give the Mill "very much a fresh start". Chief Minister Miles Walker explained that the Council of Ministers initial reaction when reviewing the report was to close the Mill but they had been persuaded to reverse this decision as a financial improvement had been forecast if new machinery was installed. Additionally strategic needs and the valuable employment provided tipped the scales in favour of retention. Of this funding, the intention was to spend just over £200,000 on new equipment and modernisation works, £50,000 on bulk loading vehicles and associated equipment and the balance to restructure the working capital and reduce the company's overdraft. The new machinery would produce flour from soft wheat which the Manx farmers would be encouraged to grow. During the debate, one member of Tynwald suggested that a new mill should be constructed on a more accessible site. Government responsibility for the Mill passed to Department of Trade and Industry in 1988.

Following his appointment as miller, Derek Osborn had found that the milling machinery was in a poor condition and breakages were common; the two wooden Henry Simon Ltd sifters on the top floor were typical and were continually leaking flour. A management team

Miller Derek Osborn with bags of flour on the roller flour.

Photo collection Andrew Scarffe.

consisting of Noel Cringle, Denis Tooley, David Corlett and Derek Osborn began the planning of a phased upgrade to the milling machinery. During October 1988, a tender from Henry Simon Ltd to carry out the work at a cost of £250,000 was approved. At this time, the machinery was still driven by line shaft, pulleys and belts, one large motor on the ground floor driving the bottom half of the mill and a second motor on the second floor operating the top two floors. A new sifter was installed on the top floor, a new purifier on the second floor and a new pneumatic lifting system was installed to replace the old belt-driven elevators and screw conveyors all of which dated to 1949. The new sifter and purifier were driven by integral electric motors allowing the removal of the old line shafts. Removal of the old equip-

Some of the Mill staff, May 1990: left to right: David Cottier, David Towers, Richard Sanderson, Derek Osborn (Mill Manager), Albert Fleming, Eddie Greason, Charlotte Smith and Roy Cormode.

ment and installation of the new equipment was completed in six weeks, Derek Osborn working closely with the team from Henry Simon Ltd on the design and installation work. As much of the work as possible was carried out by local companies including SAT Systems of Kirk Michael, BMK Electrical and J W Welding of Douglas. Before proper production began, baking tests of the flour milled from the new system were carried out by Ramsey Bakery Ltd, who reported that they were very pleased with the quality of the flour produced.

The close affinity between the mill and its principal customer, Ramsey Bakery, was exemplified in November 1988 when the mill commenced deliveries of flour to the bakery in bulk form by means of a dedicated flour tanker which blew flour from its cylindrical hold

November 1988 saw the purchase by the Mill of a bulk flour tanker to carry out deliveries to Ramsey Bakery where it blew flour into their new silo.

Photo, Andrew Scarffe.

into a new silo installed at the bakery. The delivery method was not innovative as it had been operated in the UK for many years, but it was the first of its kind on the Island and, in 1989, the Board were able to report increases in flour sales as a result. The Mill Board had been expanded during 1988 with the appointment of UK based Mr M R Dancy who was a supplier of raw materials to the mill and in welcoming him to the Board, the Chairman invited Mr Dancy to express his frank opinions on the company's operations. Sales, particularly those of animal feeds, continued to be difficult and worries were expressed at meetings of the Board over the Company's financial position. David Corlett had left the mill in 1988 and Derek Osborn assumed the role of manager and miller; the following year brought the sad news of the death of Mr Tooley in December.

Although there was an improvement in the morale of the Mill's staff following the successful improvements carried out, the government, as the Mill's sole shareholder, had also been expressing similar concerns about the Mill's financial performance. During December, 1989, the Department of Trade and Industry instructed the Board to close the animal feed plant with immediate effect. The instruction directly opposed the intentions of the Board who were intent upon improving the plant and, in the process, its profitability. Nevertheless, the instruction was carried out.

On 14th December 1989, the Department of Trade and Industry

Minister made the shock public announcement that the animal feed-stock department was to close completely and fifteen staff were to be made redundant. Mr May told members of Tynwald that the operation was losing £180,000 per year and that *"examination of the company's trading performance has shown the animal feedstock to be a loss making activity and the situation cannot be allowed to continue. Recent investigations have revealed a need for further urgent capital investment in the plant and machinery if production of feed is to carry on and such investment cannot be justified by the future prospects of the mill. The first priority is to safeguard the flour milling side of the business".*

Mr May stressed that there was no intention of closing the flour mill and it was stated that there were several other suppliers of animal feeds on the Island.

The decision was greeted with both anger and dismay by the Mill workforce, their union, the people of Laxey and throughout the Island. Former director Dr Edgar Mann branded the timing of the decision as "callous", having been made immediately before Christmas with no prior warning being given to the staff involved.

Unpalatable as this decision was at the time, particularly to those who had lost their jobs, with the benefit of hindsight it is highly likely that the decision to close the animal feedstock manufacture at this time prevented the complete closure of the Mill in later years.

As a result, the relationship between the Board and the government deteriorated and, on 23rd August 1990 at a fractious morning meeting, the Board were informed by representatives of the DTI that they were to be replaced at the Annual General Meeting to be held later that day. At the AGM, the board strongly protested at the manner in which their service at the company had been terminated. Their discontent was noted, but their replacement went ahead and Mr Henry Robinson and Mr Ray Kniveton were appointed to the Board. Both men brought with them a wealth of business experience. Mr Kniveton was a director and later owner of the successful coach business Tours (Isle of Man). Mr Robinson, or "Robbie" as he was almost universally known, had spent his working career within the Manx agriculture industry, having set up the Isle of Man Agricultural Marketing Society in 1959 and the Isle of Man Dairy in the 1960s. He had retired in 1985 but had been persuaded by the shareholders to join the Board and was appointed Chairman during September 1990.

Both directors were present in the public gallery of Tynwald in December 1990 to hear members agree to "wipe the slate clean" and vote £208,000 to meet the operating deficit incurred by the Mill during

H. T. "Robbie" Robinson, left, and Ray Kniveton, later to become MHK for Onchan, were appointed in August 1990 with a brief to make the Mill profitable or close it.

the financial year ending 31st March 1990. Members of Tynwald were told that a large proportion of this deficit was to write off bad debts and meet redundancy payments and that the new directors were confident of taking the mill into an era of profitability.

The new directors were given a simple brief by Government; to either make the mill profitable or close it down. A business plan was drawn up to identify a modernisation process which would be implemented over the next few years to place the Mill on a more secure financial footing. The animal feed plant closure was carried out and the equipment was disposed of. A new management structure was put in place to improve efficiency and to introduce new hygiene and health and safety standards. It was identified that with further capital expenditure, additional efficiencies could be obtained from the recently modernised milling equipment. All other aspects of the milling process were examined and over the next decade renewals and repairs were made to the mill building, the machinery and storage facilities. A number of unoccupied properties owned by the Mill but which were deemed to be of no further use were sold to release capital. Other parts of the mill which were unused were leased to provide rental revenue and with income from these sources, together with a number of grants from the Department of Industry, further expenditure on machinery and equipment could be carried out while profitability was maintained.

A need for additional storage capacity was identified and an order was placed during December, 1990 for two new galvanized silos each capable of storing 650 tonnes of wheat. These were constructed in 1991; one of the older silos dating to the early 1970s was demolished in 1992. During 1990 Nigel Mahoney was appointed assistant miller and quality controller. He had previously been employed at Spillers in Birkenhead with Derek Osborn. Like millers of old, it is said Nigel could carry out an accurate quality check on grain merely by looking

The two new grain silos in the course of construction, 1991.

Grain silos (Nos 3 and 4) in the foreground with a capacity each of 650 tonnes. Silo No 1 (background) was installed in 1996.

at it! He was fascinated by all aspects of milling and made numerous notes of the changes made to the mill at the time. His untimely and premature death a few years later was a great shock to his family and friends and a major loss to the Mill.

A refurbishment of the screen house was carried out in 1991 and a second hand ripple sifter was supplied by Nelstrops of Stockport. In the mill, the line shaft driving the rollers was removed and replaced by individual electric motors installed on the ceiling of the basement, directly beneath each roller. Computerised weighing scales were introduced and a new laboratory for testing and analysing the wheat was constructed in 1993. At a ceremony held in November, Dr Edgar Mann MHK performed the official commissioning of newly-installed semi-automatic machinery for filling retail bags of flour.

Nigel Mahoney.

The Italian-made machinery was able to fill 20 packs of flour per minute tended by one person; previously three people had been employed to fill the sacks by hand. A new weighbridge was commissioned in the mill yard in 1996, to weigh both incoming wagons of wheat and deliveries of flour to bakeries. A third storage silo was construc-ted.

One of the greatest difficulties to be overcome was the cost of importing wheat from the United Kingdom as, at the time, only a small amount of milling wheat was being grown on the Island. Robbie persuaded the Department of Agriculture to operate a Milling Wheat Scheme which would offer incentives to Manx farmers to grow wheat

Peter Oates, recently retired from senior management in Isle of Man Bank, was appointed to the chair to follow Henry Robinson.

through the payment of a milling wheat bonus. The scheme would ensure that wheat was grown to a high quality and that farmers would be recompensed for the lower yields which would result when compared to other crops such as barley. No extra expense to Government was involved as there would be no requirement to pay subsidies to assist farmers in exporting barley and the mill avoided the high importation costs. The scheme proved to be extremely successful and in 1994 the Mill used 1500 tons of Manx produced wheat. By 1995 this had risen to 1,915 tons and to 2,500 tons in 1996, almost enough for the Mill's annual requirement. There was insufficient storage capacity for such volumes and a new 700-ton storage silo was constructed in 1998.

In 1994 Ray Kniveton was elected as a member of the House of Keys for Onchan and retired from the Board and Mr Peter Oates, a retired senior manager of the Isle of Man Bank, was appointed in his place. In 1997, Marks and Spencer Ltd approved the Mill's new hygiene regime for the use of the flour in bread specially made by Ramsey Bakery for their stores.

Between 1991 and 1998 AGM, when Henry Robinson retired from the Board, Laxey Glen Mills Ltd had spent approximately £1m on the re-equipment programme, most of which had been generated by the Mill itself. During the same period the company had made a profit of almost £500,000 and paid regular dividends to the Government. A profit of £89,158 had been returned during the financial year ending

March 1998. On retiring, Henry Robinson modestly noted that anyone with a small amount of business sense could have achieved the same success. Nevertheless, he and his fellow directors had turned round a loss making business and was able to pay back a dividend, albeit a relatively small one, to the taxpayer via the government who had supported the mill through earlier troubled times. Just prior to Robbie's departure Mr Colin Brown, originally from Laxey and heavily involved in the local printed media scene, was appointed to the board.

Peter Oates was appointed chairman at the 1998 AGM and he was determined that the secure financial base established by "Robbie" would be maintained. During 1999, the Mill recorded net profits of £95,000 but Mr Oates warned cheap bread imported by supermarkets could once again threaten the mill's financial viability. The level of cash reserves now enabled consideration to be given to the replacement of the 1949 Henry Simon mill rolls which were the last remaining major pieces of equipment which required replacement., Although still in operation, after nearly fifty years use the rolls were well overdue for replacement. It was now impossible to source spares and these had to be made in the mill's workshop. Machinery from Beaulieu of Switzerland; Braibanti Golfetto of Padova, Italy; Henry Simon Ltd and Thomas Robinson of Rochdale (both of which had been merged and taken over by the Japanese company Satake in 1991) were evaluated. The Golfetto machinery proved to be ideal for Laxey and the company were awarded the £300,000 contract for the installation of six new roll units. The new state-of-the-art milling equipment was commissioned at a special ceremony on 21st June, 1999 when former chairman Henry Robinson unveiled a commemorative plaque.

Regular visits to the mill by Manxman, the late John Taggart, a long-term and highly-skilled director of Rank Hovis, UK-based flour manufacturers, inevitably resulted in congratulations to all Mill staff on the quality and colour of Laxey flour - John maintained it was of considerably higher quality than any available within the UK.

The next few years saw steady growth with close co-operation being established between the mill, its suppliers and its main customer, Ramsey Bakery. A branch of the major UK supermarket chain, Tesco, had opened up operations in Douglas and had installed an in-store bakery which boosted flour sales by around 100 tonnes each year, thus adding to the annual income. However, the bakery activities of Tesco were not to last and in 2005 the company decided to close the bakery

Sandra Donnelly was appointed quality controller in 2001. In 2006, she was awarded the NABIM bronze medal which was presented by Hon Alex Downie, Minister DTI. Sandra took over the management of the company in late 2008.

operation and instead "bake-off" their products from imported part-baked or frozen dough.

Following the sad and premature death of Nigel Mahoney, Mrs Sandra Donnelly, a trained microbiologist previously employed within the dairy sector, joined the company in 2001 as quality controller and immediately established a particular interest in the milling industry and all of the associated works. Through the Mill's membership of the National Association of British and Irish Millers, Sandra enrolled on their courses to attain full milling qualifications. Her interest and enthusiasm bore fruit and at the end of the course, she was designated by NABIM as the winner of their Bronze Medal as the second best new miller throughout the Association's world-wide membership. Sandra was presented with her medal by Alex Downie, then Minister for Trade and Industry, in November 2006.

2002 saw the retirement of Peter Oates and the appointment to the Board of Mr Bob Briercliffe, former senior accountant in the Isle of

The current Board of Laxey Glen Mills Limited took office in 2002 and consists of (back) Michael Henthorn, Fred Newton (Company Secretary), Bob Briercliffe and (front) Colin Brown (Chairman), with Sandra Donnelly (Manager).

Man Government Treasury and Mr Michael Henthorn, a local businessman who was heavily involved in the local insurance sector and an official of the Isle of Man Chamber of Commerce. This membership constitutes the present Board of the Mill.

Interestingly, Bob Briercliffe had represented the government in the take-over of the Mill in 1974 and had served a short period as a director in the newly-formed company during that year. Colin Brown's other business commitments prevented him, in the short term, from taking over the Chairmanship and, as a result, Bob Briercliffe was appointed.

Derek Osborn left the Mill in May 2004 and Sandra Donnelly took over the technical responsibilities with the company and since that time has graduated to become the manager of the company as a whole. She quickly gained in stature and is highly regarded by both customers and staff alike.

Development since 2002 had been concentrated upon the stabilisation of the company's financial position and on continuing attempts to broaden the customer base. As his other commitments eased, Colin Brown took over as chairman in October 2004 working closely with Bob Briercliffe who, in turn, concentrated his involvement on the company's wheat intake and stock situation.

Ramsey Bakery remains the principal customer of the Mill and takes delivery of approximately 30 tons of flour each week thus purchasing all of its weekly flour requirement from Laxey. Situated on the former steam railway station at Ramsey, the bakery, which employs 70 people, operates throughout the day, seven days a week for 360 days a year. It is at its busiest throughout the night shift when bread is baked for delivery throughout the Island the following day. Its most popular product is the "White and Healthy" loaf which has high fibre and protein content and low levels of carbohydrates. The bakery principal, James Duncan, displays strong support for the Mill evidenced many times through assistance with sample bakings and and advisory assistance during difficult periods.

The provenance of the Mill's flour, its recognised quality and the

The support of James Duncan, principal of Ramsey Bakery along with his wife Caroline, has been invaluable to the Mill on many occasions and the Mill are proud to advertise the fact that Laxey flour is used in all of the bakery's products, delivered freshly-baked to retail outlets every day.

absence of additives which must, under UK directives be added to all flours (including organic) which are milled in the United Kingdom, have made the Isle of Man product particularly attractive to the small UK-based artisan baker. Attendance by the Mill as an exhibitor at the annual Bakers' Fair has produced a number of sales leads some of which have materialised into deliveries now being regularly made to the Midlands and to the Cumbria areas. The possibility of expanding sales to the UK is now a major aim for the Mill.

However, perhaps the biggest achievement of the lifetime of Laxey Glen Mills is the excellent working relationship which has developed between the milling wheat growers, the Mill and the Manx baking industry. This tripartite operation ensures the livelihood of around 15 farmers and their families, eight milling operatives and their families, around 100 staff and families at Ramsey Bakery and a further 20 or so families whose principals are engaged in the industry.

As the Mill now begins its second 150 years, it does so from the most secure financial and mechanical position enjoyed for many decades. The greatest threat to its future viability remains, as ever, the importation of cheaply produced bread into the Manx market. Every one of us, in some way, has a connection with the Mill be it as consumers of bread and pastries; as purchasers of flour; as producers and suppliers; as employees; as bakers and as the people of the Isle of Man in whom ownership of the Mill is ultimately vested. It is up to each and every one of us to continue our support of this unique asset, the Laxey Glen Mills.

~ 4 ~

FODEN - LGM LEGEND

For almost seventy years, the immaculately presented and maintained Foden lorries, used for delivering animal foods to the Island's farmers and flour to bakeries and shops, were a familiar sight on the Island's roads. Although other makes of lorries were at times owned and used, it is the Fodens which are still fondly remembered today.

The first mechanical delivery vehicle to be owned by the Mill was a Foden steam wagon; it was one of the very first steam wagons to be used on the Island. Registered as MN 362 on 8th April, 1913 it had an unladen weight of 4 tons 18 cwt and was painted "vermillion picked out in blue". Used primarily for delivering flour and animal feeds to the Mill's warehouse on North Quay in Douglas, it enabled some of

No photograph is known to exist of the Mill's two Foden steam wagons. However, they would have been almost identical to this Foden belonging to the Isle of Man Highway Board.

Photo collection, Andrew Scarffe.

the deliveries carried out by traditional horse and cart to be dispensed with. While the purchase of the lorry showed that the Mill was keen to use the most up-to-date road transport available at the time, unfortunately the condition of the Island's roads were not quite as

The last of the Fodens, YMN 741 purchased in 1959 and photographed shortly before withdrawal in 1981. The vehicle is now preserved on the Island.

Photo Andrew Scarffe.

advanced. Entirely unforeseen consequences were to follow in 1917 when the Mill was held responsible by the Isle of Man Highway Board for damage caused to the main Douglas to Laxey road.

The case was heard at the Douglas Courthouse on 22nd October 1917, when the Highway Board sought to recover £517 1s 10d which it was alleged *"was the amount expended on the Douglas to Laxey Road from April 1913 to November 1915 over and above the ordinary expenditure of the upkeep of the road, such extraordinary expenditure allegedly caused by the defendants Foden steam wagon"*. In addition to local advocates and witnesses, four highway engineers from England were present to give evidence for either the plaintiffs or defendants.

Prior to 1913, the condition of the road was said to be exceptionally good and traffic consisted of horse vehicles, light motors and the occasional traction engine towing threshing mills between farms. In November 1913, the Board's Surveyor General first drew attention to the "considerable damage" to the road through Lonan and Onchan caused by the steam wagon which was making two return journeys between Laxey and Douglas each day. The allegation was refuted at the time by the Mill whose expert witnesses were of the opinion that the

Fodens KMN 184 purchased in 1948 and LMN 253 purchased in 1949 pose outside the mill in centenary year, 1960.

Photo collection, Andrew Scarffe.

soft nature of the road and inferior quality of the stone was totally inadequate for any real traffic. By January 1916, the Surveyor General noted that the road had deteriorated rapidly and 400 tons of stone were required for its repair. During September, the defendants were sent an account for the expenditure carried out on repair work; the account was disputed and the legal proceedings followed.

James Corteen, Parochial Surveyor of Highways for the parishes of Lonan and Maughold stated that before 1913 the road was always well maintained with stones from the Laxey Mine used as a foundation and granite macadam (the granite was sourced from the Dhoon and Santon) as a top coating. In his opinion the steam wagon had caused the deterioration which had caused the surface of the road to be pushed to the sides on the corners and corrugations elsewhere.

Mr Thomas Davies, an engineer from Foden, presented evidence on behalf of the Mill. It was noted that the wagon could be driven at a speed of eight miles per hour although the usual speed was about six miles per hour. With a full load, the total weight would be 12 tons. The Mill's advocate argued that the Highway Board was bound to maintain the highway in proper condition, no matter what the cost and no matter what the traffic. Unfortunately for the Mill, the High Bailiff did not agree and damages were awarded to the Board, although this was reduced to £275. Almost immediately, the Foden steam wagon was offered for sale and was eventually sold to a company based in Warrington in February, 1918.

Six years were to elapse before the Mill purchased another steam wagon. Again supplied by Foden the wagon was registered as MN 3195 on 25th May 1924. Painted in a "chocolate" livery, the wagon had an unladen weight of 6 tons 18 cwt and a maximum speed of 12 mph. With solid wheels, twin at the rear and improved rubbed tyres, the new wagon fortunately did not damage the roads as its predecessor had done. However, it was to last less than two years with the Mill

Children enjoy a ride on the rear of YMN 741 during delivery of animal feed to a Bride farm.

Photo Michael Leece.

71

before being transferred to Corlett Sons and Cowley Ltd on North Quay, Douglas in April 1926.

It was to be another nine years before the Laxey Glen Mill purchased another vehicle. MAN 558, a Ford van, was registered in September 1935 but was to remain with the Mill for less than three years. It was, however, the first vehicle to carry the familiar white livery with red lettering. It is not clear how deliveries were made during the intervening years although R G Corlett Ltd made considerable use of the Manx Electric Railway; a proposal to build a steeply graded branch line from the railway to the mill had not been pursued. R G Corlett had purchased two lorries for the Eureka Mills at Ramsey and may have had the use of the vehicles belonging to Corlett Sons and Cowley Ltd. It would seem unlikely, by this time, that horse and cart were used.

The next lorry was a Guy Vixon purchased in November 1936 and registered BMN 571, which remained in service until August 1938. A Thorneycroft CMN 585 followed in September 1937 and was notable as the first diesel engine lorry to be operated by the mill. A Bedford lorry EMN 121 was acquired in November 1939 before a return was made to a Foden chassis when EMN 547 was purchased in November 1940. This was joined by an identical vehicle EMN 680 in March 1941 and both gave over 12 years service to the Mill.

The first new lorry purchased after the end of the Second World War was KMN 184 another Foden, purchased in October 1948 but now fitted with a 36.5 HP diesel engine. It is recalled that this vehicle was notable for the copious volumes of black exhaust produced by the engine, a characteristic which was finally solved by Edgar Kinrade following his purchase of the vehicle. Edgar sold KMN 184 to Manx Plant

LMN 253, purchased in 1949, parked outside the mill and fully loaded with sacks of animal feed. The delivery men had to manually load and unload the wagons.

Photo collection, John Kneale.

3342 MN, purchased in 1961, was the sole Seddon owned by the Mill.

Photo Michael Leece.

Ltd of Ramsey who, it is said, removed the engine and sent it to India for use on a boat. LMN 253 followed in July 1949, PMN 208 in March 1953 and YMN 741 in March 1959. The two-stroke diesel engine fitted to the latter wagon was notoriously noisy and conversation in the cab was recalled as being near impossible. Although the 1960 Mill centenary supplement recorded the long association with Foden and the four Foden wagons were posed for publicity photographs, no further vehicles of this make were purchased and the next wagon was a Seddon.

The final two wagons were to be of the ubiquitous Bedford TK chassis. Both had platform bodies although a separate box and conveyor were later purchased to mount on each to enable loose grain to be carried. Following the delivery of 731 TMN, PMN 208 was returned to Foden for refurbishment the cost of which, it is believed, was equivalent to the purchase price of a new Bedford TK. Although it would seem sensible to have purchased a further Bedford, the refur-

The last two wagons purchased by RG Corlett Ltd were the ubiquitous Bedford TK chassis. Michael Leece is pictured with brand new 731 TMN after having won "Driver of the Year" award.

Photo Michael Leece

PMN 208 was decorated with a model of Laxey Wheel and took part in a parade through Laxey village to celebrate the centenary of the wheel in September, 1954.

Photos collection, Andrew Scarffe.

(Below) Following sale by the Mill, PMN 208 was preserved on the Island for a short period. It is pictured here on Peel Promenade.

Photo Andrew Scarffe.

(Below) PMN 208 was returned to Foden for refurbishment in 1970. Following completion of the work, the wagon was posed next to Laxey Wheel for publicity photographs. Russell Henry stands proudly by the wagon.

Photo collection Chris Wedgwood.

Bedford TK 731 TMN being loaded with sacks of animal foods outside the Isle of Man Steam Packet's warehouse at Douglas harbour, in 1988.

Photo Andrew Scarffe.

bishment undoubtedly contributed to the Foden's longevity. PMN 208 and its younger sister YMN 741 were both finally taken out of service in the early 1980s. Fortunately both found new homes with preservationists Les and Dave Gleave of Baldrine, but were later sold off-Island. In spring 2009, YMN 741 was repatriated by Chris

Wedgwood who had, during the previous year, completed the restoration of a 1934 Sentinel steam wagon. In April 2010, PMN 208 was offered for sale in a commercial vehicle auction in Cambridge and was purchased by Chris Wedgwood and Mark Edwards. YMN 741 was fully restored to R G Corlett Ltd condition for the Mill's 150th anniversary.

During the mid-1980s, bulk deliveries of animal feeds began using these specially acquired Leyland wagons.

Photos Andrew Scarffe.

Details of all the known vehicles used by Laxey Glen Mill up to nationalisation in 1974. While believed to be complete, any further information or amendments would be gratefully received.

MN 362 Foden Steam Wagon   New April 1913
Disposed February 1918 to a Warrington based operator.

MN 3195 Foden Steam Wagon   New May 1924
Disposed April 1926 to Corlett Sons and Cowley Ltd, Douglas.

MAN 558 8HP Ford Van   New September 1935
Disposed April 1938 to R Shooter, Agneash

BMN 571 20HP Guy Vixen lorry   New November 1936
Disposed May 1941 to F Orrell, Ridgeway Street, Douglas

CMN 385 30HP Thornycroft diesel lorry   Purchased s/hand Sept 1937
Disposed October 1940 to A Tapsell, Strand St, Douglas.

DMN 504 10HP Bedford van   New February 1939
Disposed February 1941 to Cox's Motors, Strand Street, Douglas

EMN 121 28 HP Bedford Lorry   New November, 1939
Registration cancelled November 1940

EMN 547 22.5HP Foden diesel lorry   New November 1940
Registration cancelled November 1952

EMN 680 22.5HP Foden diesel lorry   New March 1941
Registration cancelled April 1953

BMN 271 30 HP Ford lorry   New June 1936
Purchased April, 1944 (RGC Ltd was the 4th owner)
Disposed June 1946 to L Christian, Ballaoates Pig Farm

FMN 929 28 HP Bedford lorry   New November 1944
Disposed March 1946 to Milntown Manufacturing, Douglas

KMN 184 36.5HP Foden lorry diesel   New October 1948
Disposed June 1961 to E A Kinrade, Laxey - converted to a tipper

KMN 804 30HP Fordson lorry   New March 1949
Disposed September 1952 to D Watterson , Athol Street, Douglas

LMN 253 22,5 HP Foden lorry   New July, 1949
Disposed May 1963 to D Fletcher, Hawarden Avenue, Douglas

PMN 208 22.5 HP Six ton Foden lorry   New March, 1953
Sold October, 1981 to L & B Magee, Baldrine then to Les and Dave Gleave, Baldrine for preservation. Purchased in UK by Chris Wedgwood and Mark Edwards, April 2010 - returned to IOM for preservation.

YMN 741 2.5Ltr 2-str diesel Foden lorry   New March, 1959
Sold 1982 to L & B Magee, Baldrine then to Les and Dave Gleave, Baldrine for preservation. Sold to UK-based preservationist. Returned to IOM by Chris Wedgwood in Spring 2009 and restored to R G Corlett condition.

3342 MN 5000cc Seddon.   New April, 1961.
Withdrawal date unknown. Eventually passed to Charles Kerruish, farmer, and used to carry hay bales.

3713 MN 1390cc Commer Cob van.   New June, 1961.

7061 MN 4297cc Bedford TK, 7 ton, flat back. New March, 1963.
Withdrawal date unknown. Eventually passed to Edgar Kinrade, Laxey and cannibalised for spares.

731 TMN Bedford TK, 7 ton, flat back. New 1970.
Withdrawal date unknown. Believed to have passed to a Douglas based scaffolding company.

Photo, Stuart Bridson

Aconspicuous feature on the front of the mill is the tablet, mounted at roof level, which contains the date of construc- tion and an emblem depicting a lamb and a flag. It has often been claimed that this emblem is Richard Rowe's family crest but it is in fact a Christian symbol with origins which reach almost as far back as the dawn of Christianity. In Christian symbolism, the Paschal Lamb, as it is known, represents Christ as the Lamb of God; such a representation of Christ as a lamb is known as an Agnus Dei. From the time of the Middle Ages, when it was adopted as the symbol of the Knights Templar, the lamb was shown standing with a banner rep- resenting Christ risen and triumphant over death. Around this time the symbol was also adopted by wool manufacturers as a sign of purity of their product. In the eighteenth and nineteenth centuries, Cornish tin mines similarly adopted the emblem as a sign of purity of the tin; ingots were stamped with the emblem before export. A use somewhat out of keeping with the emblem's origins was by public houses throughout Britain; the "Lamb and Flag" was a fairly common name and one such named public house existed in Douglas for a short while.

Various Rowe families, from as far apart as Devon and Yorkshire, adopted the Lamb and Flag emblem as their family crest including, it would seem, Richard Rowe; the emblem is therefore not specific to his family. However, as a sign of purity, it is a particularly apt emblem for the Laxey Glen Mill and its products.

—❦ 5 ❦—

IOM WHEAT INTO IOM FLOUR

Wheat, in common with other cereals such as oats, rye and barley, are all types of farinaceous grasses; farinaceous literally means flour producing. Wheat is one of the most common cereal crops grown worldwide and in the United Kingdom alone approximately 16 million tonnes are grown each year. There are many varieties of wheat, some of which are suitable for use as animal feeds and others which are better suited for milling into flour. Of the latter, there are two types, hard or soft, which describe the texture of the endosperm. Hard wheat has a high gluten content and is used to make bread and fine cakes. The softer varieties tend to be used in pastries and biscuits.

Unripened wheat presents a glorious shade of green. The Mill uses only Manx wheat grown on the Island's northern plain.

Wheat is an annual plant which means that it grows from seed, flowers, produces its own seed and then dies in one year. This means that some of the seed or grain has to be saved from one harvest to grow the following year's crop. An individual wheat grain is one of the seeds which the plant forms to reproduce itself. A single wheat stalk produces between twenty and fifty grains dependent on the variety.

A grain of wheat is typically between five and eight millimeters long and consists of three main parts. Bran is the hard outer coat, consisting of a number of layers, which protects the seed from damage from the weather or when it is in the soil; it is an excellent source of fibre. The germ is found

The ripening wheat takes on a different colour prior to harvest when it is cut and stalks are separated from the wheat grain.

at one end of the grain and is the part which would become the plant if the seed was allowed to germinate or grow. During the milling process it is removed as it can cause flour to go rancid during storage. The endosperm is the food reserve that the young plant consumes from germination until it has grown sufficient roots to enable nutrients to be picked up from the soil. It accounts for 83 per cent of the weight of the grain and is the source of the white flour. It consists mainly of starch but also contains proteins called gliadin and glutelin.

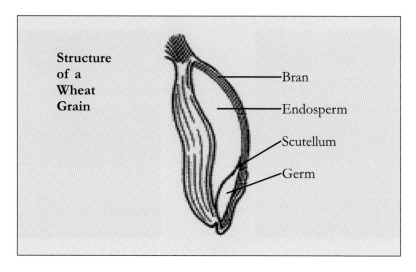

Structure of a Wheat Grain

Bran
Endosperm
Scutellum
Germ

These proteins interact to produce gluten which helps to make dough rise, giving bread a light, fine texture.

The millers job is to separate out the various parts of the wheat grain and to make a fine powdery flour; a single grain of wheat makes about 20,000 particles of flour. The modern roller system of milling breaks open the grain and separates out the various parts in progressive stages called gradual reduction, the "intermediate stock" being sifted and screened between each stage which results in a very fine white flour. To make wholemeal flour, the parts of the grain which were previously removed are added back in. Apart from the introduction of rollers to replace millstones, the basic principle of milling has remained unchanged; Thomas Corlett would be entirely familiar with the milling principles and techniques still in use at the mill today.

There are currently thirteen Manx farmers, all farming on the "northern plain" of the Island, who in total grow and supply approximately 2500 tons of wheat to the Mill each year. The crop is either sown between late September and November as "winter wheat" which is harvested in mid-August, or is sown between February and April as "spring wheat" for harvesting in September. Winter wheat gives a bigger yield and produces about three tons per acre.

Wheat suitable for milling and bread making is an expensive commodity to grow in comparison to wheat grown for animal feeds, due to the fertilisers which are used. There is a greater financial reward for the farmer at harvest time but this has to be balanced against a much greater risk should the crop fail for any reason, such as bad weather.

Under such circumstances the loss is borne entirely by the farmer as the mill makes no interim payment. However, a damaged crop may still be suitable for animal feed though, as such, provides a lower income.

About a year before harvest, the mill and the farmers agree contracts for the supply of wheat. Terms and conditions specified in the contract include a target tonnage and the acreage of land upon which the wheat will be grown. When harvested, the wheat must be free from sprouted grain, disease, stones and animal waste and meet minimum standards of moisture and protein content.

Harvesting usually begins in mid-August. A combine harvester cuts the wheat ears off the stalks and an internal a series of rollers and presses separates the grain which is ejected into a hopper on the rear of the machine. When the hopper is full the grain is transferred into trailers and taken to a large dryer which are similar to a giant domestic tumbler dryer. The dryer reduces the moisture content of the grain but it is very important that the grain is not subjected to prolonged drying as this damages the protein content. Meanwhile, the remaining wheat stalks are cut by a baler and made into large cylindrical bales which are used as animal feed during the winter months.

As harvesting progresses, the farmer provides the mill with an estimated crop tonnage and samples are sent to the mill for testing. Once the samples are tested and accepted a collection schedule is agreed, the mill being responsible for all transport arrangements and

The mill laboratory where samples of grain are tested before delivery and samples of flour are tested throughout the milling process.

Photo, Andrew Scarffe

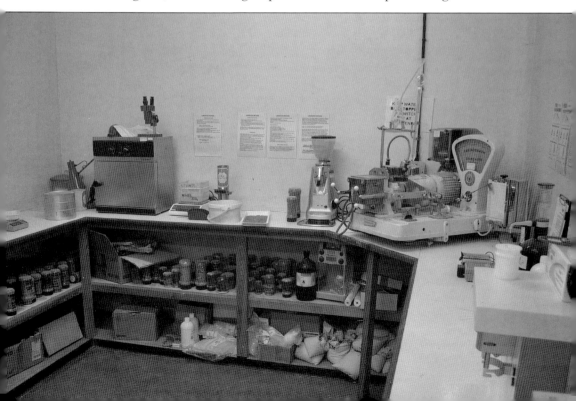

costs. Occasionally, a farmer may be requested to store some wheat on his farm, for which an extra payment is made, but all wheat is normally scheduled to be collected by the mill by the end of December.

Wheat is collected from the farmers in tipper wagons. On arriving at the mill, the wagon is parked on the weighbridge and weighed. Before the load is accepted, a number of tests are carried out in the mill's own laboratory on a sample taken from the load. This takes about twenty minutes which gives sufficient time for the driver to have a mug of tea or coffee! To take the sample, a spear with collecting lugs is driven into the load, ensuring that a representative sample of the entire load is obtained. The sample is placed in a bucket and shaken. A visual examination is carried out for disease, insect or vermin damage and the colour and smell are examined. Samples of impure, diseased or damaged wheat are kept in jars in the lab to be used as comparisons. A small amount of the wheat is then ground into a powder and placed into a machine to undergo a Near Infrared scan or NIR. Within seconds a full analysis of the protein content, moisture content and hardness is produced on a print out; the test may be carried out a number of times. Minimum acceptable standards for each of these properties are required. If there is too much moisture present the wheat may decompose in the silos. In such an instance, further drying can be carried out by the farmer and the load can then be resubmitted. A further sample of the wheat is sieved to extract any weed seeds; if there are large quantities of weed seeds present the payment to the farmer will be reduced, although these are removed during the screening process. Wheat with lower protein content can be accepted provided the minimum standard is still achieved as additional gluten can be added into the flour during the milling process. This is a completely natural additive and is purchased from mills

One of the most important qualities of wheat is its ability to be milled into flour with a "good Hagberg" which assists greatly in the production of bread. Hagberg quality is tested by this simple machine.

Photo, Andrew Scarffe

82

The 1956 extension with its flat roof is clearly evident in this photograph taken from the entrance to the Laxey Glen Gardens. The pipe leading from the second floor window is used to load flour into the bulk delivery tanker.

Photo, Andrew Scarffe.

which specialise in gluten production. Plain flour used for baking pastries does not require as high gluten content as the flour used in bread making.

One of the most important tests carried out on the grain is known as the Hagberg Falling Number or HFN. This measures the presence of an enzyme in the grain which assists the seed with germination. If the level of the enzyme in the grain is too high, the grain may sprout during storage and if the germination process has started, the quality of the flour is reduced. To carry out the test, a weighed sample of ground wheat is mixed with water in a large test tube which is then placed in a bath of boiling water. The wheat and water forms a gel in the test tube. A plunger is placed into the test tube and the time taken for the plunger to fall though the gel is recorded. If the grain has a high enzyme activity, the gel is thinner, the plunger falls more quickly and the resultant Hagberg is low. If the Hagberg is below the minimum acceptable standard, the grain is rejected by the mill although it could still be used for other purposes such as animal foods.

Following an extremely wet summer, much of the grain from the 2008 harvest showed a very low Hagberg and failed the testing procedure. Heavy rain had flattened the crops and when the grain had come into contact with the damp ground nature's germination process had begun. As the harvested wheat was damp, a number of the farmers had subjected the grain to prolonged drying and in doing so had damaged the protein content, resulting in poor bread production. As a result, an additional testing machine was purchased for the mill laboratory to measure gluten quantity and strength. With the assistance of the Department of Agriculture, the Mill transported a machine temporarily to the Island which was able to separate out the sprouted grain by density and 1500 tons of Manx wheat was able to be saved by this method. During 2009 an additional test was introduced to detect the presence of mycotoxins in the grain. These are extremely toxic but fortunately the Isle of Man is not in a high risk area for mycotoxins although the tests still have to be carried out. All the wheat samples taken from the delivery lorries are bagged and retained, each being given a unique serial number which is cross referenced to the test results.

Samples of the flour are removed from various stages of the milling process every two hours and these are also subjected to a similar testing regime. A further machine tests the strength of the flour and dough for the correct baking qualities. Wholemeal flour is also tested by sieving flour samples.

Once the delivery of wheat has been accepted by the mill, the delivery wagon reverses into an intake area situated between the silos and offloads the wheat into the intake pit. There are four storage silos with a total capacity of 2350 tons. At least 600 tons of wheat or flour has to be kept at the mill as part of the Strategic Food Reserve. The wheat is sorted into the silos dependent on its protein content. Currently, three of the silos are used for storing wheat with lower protein content and one for storing wheat with higher protein content. A bucket elevator lifts the wheat from the intake pit to the gantry above the silos and it is then fed into the selected silo. Air is regularly blown into the silos to keep them cool and fresh. The temperature inside each silo is monitored daily by two separate probes which take readings throughout the full depth of the wheat. If decomposition begins, the temperature of the wheat rises.

It would be logical to expect that the wheat would enter the mill on one floor, pass through machinery on each floor in turn and then emerge on the fourth floor as flour. In fact, the milling process involves the wheat, the "intermediate stock" (as it is termed) and the flour being passed from the basement of the mill to the top floor and back again many times until all the flour has been removed from

the grain. The mill has four floors, the basement floor containing the base pipework of the various elevators and pneumatic lift and the air compressor which operates the pneumatics; the first floor containing the rollers; the second floor containing the purifiers, and the third or top floor containing the sifters, dust collector and cyclones for the pneumatic system; all floors are clean, bright and airy. The milling process is controlled by a computer located in the first floor office.

Before being milled, the wheat has to be thoroughly cleaned in the screening house. Wheat is taken from the bottom of each silo by a screw conveyor and elevator to the inside of the screen house and dropped into what is termed a "dirty bin", each silo having its own "dirty bin"; this process is called "turning". The process of cleaning the wheat and adding a small amount of moisture is known as "screening". Various machines remove impurities by their differing size, weight and shape. Metallic objects are removed by a number of magnets which are placed throughout the mill; metal fragments could cause great damage to delicate machinery. A Gravity Selector vibrates the wheat and removes any stones separating them by density; a surprisingly extremely small amount of stones gets into the wheat. A Ripple Sieve takes out

The screenhouse - where the wheat is transferred from the silos, cleaned and stored prior to milling.

Photo, Andrew Scarffe

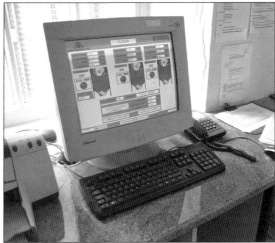

The modern milling operation, including the supply of raw wheat into the mill, is controlled by computer.

Photo, Andrew Scarffe

chaff etc by allowing the wheat to drop through wheat-sized holes through which the chaff cannot pass. Weed seeds are extracted by Carter Disc machines. These contain a row of metallic discs which have indentations to match the size of various weed seeds. The revolving discs pick up the weed seeds and the wheat grains pass straight through the machine. All machines in the screen house are powered by indi-

(Left) The roll floor with the modern Golfetto rolls and viewing "funnels". (Far left) The purifier. (Lower left) The chute used to transfer bagged flour to the loading bay.

Photos, Andrew Scarffe

(Top right) During the milling process, flour continuously passes through the sifter. (Below) The tanker supplies bulk flour to Ramsey Bakery where, using its own equipment, it blows the flour into the bakery's silos.

Photos, Andrew Scarffe

vidual electric motors. The wheat may pass through the machines in the screen house several times. By controlling the volume of wheat which is removed from each dirty bin and mixed during the screening process, the recipe mix or "grist" of the wheat to be milled is controlled.

Once it is has been cleaned the wheat passes from the top floor of the screen house onto the top floor of the mill. Here, a very small amount of water is added, usually about one per cent by volume. The moistened wheat is stored overnight in eight "clean bins", each of which have a capacity of five tons, to undergo a process called conditioning where the moisture loosens the hard outer skins of the grain. As the conditioning process takes place overnight, the screening and mixing process must take place on the day prior to milling. If required, different "grists" of wheat can be stored in the different "clean bins" to await milling.

When milling is about to begin, conditioned wheat is taken from the bottom of the relevant "clean bin" on the ground floor and lifted by elevators all the way back to the top floor. It is then weighed so an accurate record of the amount of wheat being milled is maintained, being before being dropped down into the first pair of rollers located on the roller floor.

There are six sets of rolling machines each of which contains two pairs of rollers. The first four pairs of rollers are called the "breaks" where the bran and the germ are removed and the remainder are termed the "reductions" which grind the large lumps of flour into a fine powder. Having passed through the "first break" the intermediate stock drops down to the basement where the pneumatic air system lifts it back to the top floor to the sifter which sieves out the flour. With the flour removed the stock now drops back down to the second pair of rollers called the "second break" the entire process being repeated through the "third break" and the "fourth break". At each stage flour is removed by the sifter although most of the flour from the grain is removed during the "breaks". Semolina, which consists of larger lumps of endosperm, is produced during the "break stages".

Once the sifter has removed the flour from the "fourth break", the stock is sorted by its size in the purifier; this determines which set of reduction rollers it is sent to. It is repeatedly passed through the reduction rollers, sifter and purifier until the flour particles have been reduced to the desired size. Any final lumps remaining in the flour are removed by the entoleter which is located on the second floor. Sight glasses are located above each rolling machine to show the state of the intermediate stock at its various stages; these never show pure

Bagged flour is stored on the second and third floors in the mill.

Photo, Andrew Scarffe

flour as this is removed by the sifter at each stage. The break rollers are serrated and the reduction rollers are smooth. The separation between each pair of rollers can be adjusted slightly which alters the intensity of the grind. Each roller weighs approximately half a ton and spares are kept in stock. A sample of flour is tested in the laboratory every twohours to ensure product consistency.

The sifter contains 240 separate sieves in a number of separate compartments. In each compartment, the sieves have a decreasing mesh size, the larger meshed sieves being made from metal the smaller sieves from nylon. The flour has to be able to pass through the tiny holes in the finest mesh sieves. Years ago, sieves were made from silk but, being a natural product these were often damaged by insects or decay. The finished flour is weighed to maintain an accurate production record. Sixteen tons of wheat can be milled each day, one ton of wheat producing 750kg of flour and 250kg of "wheatings" as the by-product is now termed.

Two large bins, each with a capacity of 19 tons, store the flour produced for Ramsey Bakery. These discharge into a pneumatic system on the roller floor which lifts the flour back up to the floor above and into a discharge pipe which can be connected directly onto the bulk delivery road tanker. At Ramsey bakery the tanker self-discharges by blowing out the flour into two storage silos. The tanker has a maximum capacity of approximately 19 tons of flour. All other flour is bagged, either in 32 kg or 16kg sacks for delivery to the Island's bakeries or into small 1.5 kg bags for retail sale.

To make wholemeal flour the bran and germ are re-introduced. White and wholemeal flour are kept separate to avoid cross contamination, during the mixing, packing and storage. Sacks of brown flour for commercial customers are stored on the top floor and sacks of white flour on the second floor. Each bag is sealed by hand stitching and then given a unique serial number which corresponds to the production run. For full traceability, it is possible to verify the flour from the relevant laboratory tests. Flour is currently exported to UK customers; who exclusively buy from the mill as the flour is traceable and additive free. The sacks are dropped down a spiral chute to the loading bay at the side of the ground floor for loading onto delivery wagons.

Flour which is sold on the retail market is bagged to the rear of the mill in a packing room which formerly held the diesel generator. White flour is packed automatically but the smaller volume of brown flours is bagged manually. As the two types cannot be mixed, the packing machine cannot be used to bag both types of flour. However, in a substantial capital investment, plans are afoot to centralise all packing in this area and to update the packing mechanism.

In an extension to the rear of the screening house, "screenings" such as straw and peas extracted during the screening process are crushed and mixed with the wheatings and bagged as animal feed. Rich in protein content, it is a valuable by product which is highly in demand, perhaps somewhat ironically considering the many problems which beset the old animal foodstuff operation.

As flour dust can be explosive under certain conditions, an extraction system removes the dust at each stage of the milling process and collects it in a large bin located on the top floor. In the extremely unlikely event of an explosion, a relief valve from the bin would vent through a panel located in the window adjacent to the exterior clock on the top floor.

All of the retail packs of the Mill's products have been rebranded as part of the company's anniversary celebrations. The product range now numbers 15 flour varieties.

The mill building and operations fully conform with all of the Island's health and safety regulations and food processing requirements. The milling and ancillary equipment now ensures that this example of 150-year-old Manx industry is as up-to-date and as efficient as possible and the Mill stands on a level equal to any similar operation worldwide - indeed, better than many!

TIME FOR CELEBRATION

The month of June was established as the month of Anniversary celebrations. Thursday 24th was set aside as the Informal Gathering of past members of staff who were invited to drinks in a marquee on the mill forecourt. The following day, 25th, a buffet was served to invited guests which included members of Government, customers and suppliers and Sunday 27th was designated the "Family Fun Day" with all sorts of competitions and games.

(Top) A large number of past employees met on Thursday - this commemorative photograph includes a number who are featured in the 1960 photograph on Page 44. (Clockwise from above left) At the Friday buffet lunch Henry 'Robbie' Robinson enjoyed meeting old friends; Manager Sandra Donnelly receives her bouquet from LGM Director Mike Henthorn; wife of LGM Chairman, Gwynneth Brown and Chairman of Laxey Commissioners, Sue Jones; LGM Secretary Fred Newton and Mrs Newton; Chairman of IOM Wheat Growers, Steve Martin in happy mood.

(Clockwise from top left) Geoff Corlett and Mrs Corlett with David Casement; Sandra Donnelly with LGM Director Bob Briercliffe; President of Tynwald and former LGM Chairman Noel Cringle; past and present LGM Directors; wheat grower Robert Morrey and son; growers Chris Martin and John Corlett with Ed Clague (DEFA) and Lisa Corlett; LGM Chairman Colin Brown with David Casement who unveiled the commemorative plaque; former shareholder representative Fred Kissack and current representative Mary Williams; Speaker of the Keys Steve Rodan and Paul Bloom.

(Left) LGM Chairman Colin Brown presents his address; (Below) a section of the audience; (Right) Conor Sullivan and Mrs Sullivan of the Mona Lisa restaurant, Laxey; (Bottom) the Family Fun Day on Sunday drew a big crowd and the children enjoyed the special arrangements especially the juggler and the bouncy castle.

Action from the Family Fun Day - (Clockwise from top left) preparing for the pancake race; practice makes perfect; the race gets under way; Dusty Miller was the star; one of the decorated cakes; a young guest loves her balloon; this young lad is proud of his decorated cake; it was fun for all the family; Mum's had an afternoon off!; concentration at the cake decoration. (Below) some entries in the bread-making competition; the cake made and beautifully decorated by Mrs Morphet was raffled for charity.

MILLIE

(Clockwise from above) the winners of the "Name the Tanker" competition point to her new name; LGM Director Mike Henthorn with the winner of the poster competition and her winning entry; view of the Mill yard; "Wow, Mum, it was awesome!"; the WI were busy on their stall; salt dough baking was a big hit; a test of concentration at the salt dough. (Below) some of the Victoria Sponge entries.

DIRECTORS AND MANAGEMENT OF
LAXEY GLEN MILLS LIMITED
FOLLOWING THE ACQUISITION BY IOM GOVERNMENT

	Chairman	Directors	Manager
1974	W A Crowe	J H Corlett JP	W Richardson
1975	W A Crowe	J H Corlett JP, P L Duncan, A J Winckle	W Richardson
1976	W A Crowe	J H Corlett JP, P L Duncan, A J Winckle	W Richardson
1977	W A Crowe	J H Corlett JP, P L Duncan, A J Winckle	W Richardson
1978	P L Duncan	J H Corlett JP, A J Winckle	W Richardson
1979	P L Duncan	J H Corlett JP, A J Winckle	W Richardson
1980	P L Duncan	J H Corlett JP, A J Winckle	W Richardson
1981	Dr E Mann	N Q Cringle (May)	W Richardson
1981	N Q Cringle	D H Tooley, J Radcliffe (December)	W Richardson
1982	N Q Cringle	D H Tooley, J Radcliffe	W Richardson
1983	N Q Cringle	D H Tooley, J Radcliffe	W Richardson
1984	N Q Cringle	D H Tooley, J Radcliffe	W Richardson
1985	N Q Cringle	D H Tooley, J Radcliffe	D Corlett
1986	N Q Cringle	D H Tooley, J Radcliffe	D Corlett
1987	N Q Cringle	D H Tooley, J Radcliffe	D Corlett
1988	N Q Cringle	D H Tooley, J Radcliffe, M R Dancy	D Corlett
1989	N Q Cringle	D H Tooley, J Radcliffe, M R Dancy	D Osborn
1990	H T Robinson	J R Kniveton	D Osborn
1991	H T Robinson	J R Kniveton	D Osborn
1992	H T Robinson	J R Kniveton	D Osborn
1993	H T Robinson	J R Kniveton	D Osborn
1994	H T Robinson	P R Oates	D Osborn
1995	H T Robinson	P R Oates	D Osborn
1996	H T Robinson	P R Oates	D Osborn
1997	H T Robinson	P R Oates	D Osborn
1998	P R Oates	C T Brown	D Osborn
1999	P R Oates	C T Brown	D Osborn
2000	P R Oates	C T Brown	D Osborn
2001	P R Oates	C T Brown	D Osborn
2002	R B Briercliffe	C T Brown, M H Henthorn	D Osborn
2003	R B Briercliffe	C T Brown, M H Henthorn	D Osborn
2004	C T Brown	R B Briercliffe, M H Henthorn	S Donnelly
2005	C T Brown	R B Briercliffe, M H Henthorn	S Donnelly
2006	C T Brown	R B Briercliffe, M H Henthorn	S Donnelly
2007	C T Brown	R B Briercliffe, M H Henthorn	S Donnelly
2008	C T Brown	R B Briercliffe, M H Henthorn	S Donnelly
2009	C T Brown	R B Briercliffe, M H Henthorn	S Donnelly
2010	C T Brown	R B Briercliffe, M H Henthorn	S Donnelly